BUCKNELL REVIEW

Science and Literature

Bucknell Review is a scholarly interdisciplinary journal. Each issue is devoted to a major theme or movement in the humanities or sciences, or to two or three closely related topics. The editors invite heterodox, orthodox, and speculative ideas and welcome manuscripts from any enterprising scholar in the humanities and sciences.

BUCKNELL REVIEW
A Scholarly Journal of Letters, Arts and Sciences

Editor
HARRY R. GARVIN

Associate Editor
JAMES M. HEATH

Editorial Board
PATRICK BRADY
JAMES M. HEATH
STEVEN MAILLOUX
MICHAEL D. PAYNE
JOHN WHEATCROFT

Assistants to the Editor
DOROTHY L. BAUMWOLL
JANE S. BRUMBACH

Contributors should send manuscripts with a self-addressed stamped envelope to the Editor, Bucknell University, Lewisburg, Pennsylvania 17837.

BUCKNELL REVIEW

Science and Literature

Edited by
HARRY R. GARVIN

Special Associate Editor This Issue
JAMES M. HEATH

Lewisburg
Bucknell University Press
London and Toronto: Associated University Presses

Associated University Presses, Inc.
4 Cornwall Drive
East Brunswick, NJ 08816

Associated University Presses Ltd
27 Chancery Lane
London WC2A 1NF, England

Associated University Presses
Toronto M5E 1A7, Canada

(Volume XXVII, Number 2)

Library of Congress Cataloging in Publication Data
Main entry under title:

Science and literature.

  (Bucknell review ; v. 27, no. 2)
  Includes bibliographical references.
  1. Literature and science—Addresses, essays,
lectures.   I. Garvin, Harry Raphael, 1917–
II. Heath, James M.   III. Series.
AP2.B887 vol. 27, no. 2 [PN55] 051s [801]   81-72026
ISBN 0-8387-5051-6

Printed in the United States of America

Contents

Recent Issues of *Bucknell Review*

Phenomenology, Structuralism, Semiology
Twentieth-Century Poetry, Fiction, Theory
Literature and History
New Dimensions in the Humanities and Social Sciences
Women, Literature, Criticism
The Arts and Their Interrelations
Shakespeare: Contemporary Approaches
Romanticism, Modernism, Postmodernism
Theories of Reading, Looking, and Listening
Literature, Arts, and Religion
Literature and Ideology

Notes on Contributors

JAMES M. CURTIS: Teaches at the University of Missouri–Columbia. Author of *Culture as Polyphony: An Essay on the Nature of Paradigms*, as well as numerous articles and book reviews on Russian literature and critical theory.

JAMES M. HEATH: Chairman of the Department of Classics at Bucknell University. Professional interests in Greek and Roman history, literature, and philology. Associate editor of *Bucknell Review* since 1976.

BRUCE HERZBERG: Teaches at Clark University. Compiled the annotated bibliography of Pynchon criticism in *Twentieth Century Literature* (May 1975); articles on Pynchon as well as on theory of the novel and theory of composition. In progress: a book-length study of Pynchon.

MARTIN KARLOW: Teaches at the University of Minnesota in Minneapolis. In progress: articles on Faulkner's Compson brothers and on Hawthorne's "Artist of the Beautiful." Current research: American sign language.

CHARLES KRANCE: Teaches at the University of Chicago. Publications on Céline, Beckett, Giraudoux. In progress: a book on Céline. Main professional interest: twentieth-century French fiction.

ROGER LUND: Teaches at LeMoyne College. He has written on Pope and is the editor of *Restoration and Early Eighteenth-Century English Literature: A Select Bibliography of Resource Materials*, published by MLA. He is now at work on a study of Pope and his readers from 1800 to 1900.

JOHN NEUBAUER: Teaches at the University of Pittsburgh. Author of *Bifocal Vision: Novalis' Philosophy of Nature and Disease* (1971); *Symbolismus und symbolische Logik*, on the *ars combinatoria* in modern literature (1978); *Novalis* (1980); and numerous articles. Currently working on the aesthetics of music and on literary theory in the eighteenth century. Interested primarily in the literature and the intellectual history of Germany and Europe in the eighteenth and nineteenth centuries.

KENNETH B. NEWELL: Associate Professor of English, Christopher Newport College. Has degrees in both engineering and English. He is writing a book on George Moore's Irish Renaissance fiction (1901–6), another on Conrad's *Lord Jim*. He has published books on pattern poetry and on H. G. Wells's realistic novels; articles on fiction, Conrad, George Moore, Joyce, Paul Elmer More, science fiction.

LISA STEINMAN: Teaches at Reed College. Publications: Wallace Stevens and Percy Bysshe Shelley; poems. Current interests: T. E. Hulme, Marianne Moore.

Introduction

That literature and related arts embody in various ways significant qualities of the societies that foster them is a truism. Whereas an agrarian economy, a hierarchical society, religious conflicts, and the rise to preeminence of an Alexander or Augustus have provided a focus for literature in earlier societies, the contemporary world has seen its arts and literature dominated by the practices, products, and practitioners of science and the technology it has brought in its wake. Not surprisingly, therefore, many creative artists and thinkers reflect and reflect on the tensions that science and the scientific outlook are believed to engender. Much of modern literature and related arts is characterized by a sense that humanity may be somehow diminished by a dominant and amoral science, a suspicion that free will has been replaced by determinism that operates like a machine, an anxiety that the beauty and charm of the individual and unpredictable may be standardized in a technological process and lost, and the notion that literature and the arts may be, at root, merely something analogous to science rather than different in kind and value.

The first and most instinctive response of literature to science and its offspring in our world portrays science as an alien ideology and a threat to all the arts hold dear. But a second response that gives a more positive value to science soon follows. Science is seen as lending itself to an investigation of complexity and an ordering of the disorderly. Literature and the arts aim at structure; their goal, too, is a kind of simplicity. Science may ally itself with utopianism to achieve an ideal. Clearly, much art and literature, not to mention philosophy, has this goal. The latest toys of science offer possibilities for new kinds of artistic sport and play, for poets in particular and others less concerned with the risks of the game than with the pleasure to be derived from it.

Going beyond such purely negative or positive responses, certain contemporary thinkers and critics, literary and artistic figures along with them, have attempted to formulate and

9

grapple with the fundamental issues to which science gives rise. The obvious questions—What is Science? How does it interact with literature and the arts anyway?—become preliminaries to far-reaching studies of a philosophical discourse that encompasses these two distinctively human activities.

This issue of *Bucknell Review* offers a selection of essays that discuss works illustrating all these approaches and attitudes to science. The first section contains two papers that theorize about the relations of the arts and science. John Neubauer considers science and literature as the characteristic activities of specialized practitioners and discusses recent models for describing and explaining the history and evolution of science in terms of their applicability to a similar historiography of literature. Beginning with Karl Popper's theories of science as methodology, he then considers and criticizes Thomas Kuhn's theory of science as revolutions within accepted paradigms. When he moves on to examine attempts by yet more recent scholars to refine or overturn Kuhn's theory, Neubauer finds fruitful suggestions for approaches to literary historiography. James Curtis's concern is how specifically to relate the arts and science. The analogy Lenin draws between Newtonian space-time and Marxism-Leninism leads Curtis into a study of models, paradigms, structures—"receptions" for literature and science—that culminates in his development of a linguistic paradigm that has cultural analogues.

The remaining papers engage in practical criticism of particular authors, works, and genres that can in general be distinguished by their attitude toward science. Three papers present the negative side first. Roger Lund, in dealing with early-eighteenth-century satire of the Royal Society and its supposed ideology, introduces a topic that pervades this issue, the "poem as object," or, in the Swiftian terms he discusses, *res et verba*. Analyzing the activity of Swift and other Scriblerians, Lund suggests, pointedly if unfairly, that contemporary structuralist and deconstructionist critics of a philosophico-scientific bent can be seen as latter-day Thomas Sprats and fit subjects for satire. Bruce Herzberg and Charles Krance examine how contemporary authors use the latest scientific theories as metaphors for social or personal dilemmas. Herzberg discusses Thomas Pynchon's treatment of scientific entropy as a metaphor for the death urge that characterizes modern society. He shows how Pynchon's works present characters seeking a "closed system" to fend off entropy but thereby encompassing their own deaths. Krance looks at some of Samuel Beckett's later work and sees reflected there the "black-hole theory" of astrophysics, when an individual (usually the narrator) and his language deconstruct themselves and slowly collapse. Although both authors conceptualize science as tending toward death, their creative art proceeds from this negative evaluation of science.

A more positive attitude toward science appears in the final set of papers. Martin Karlow's study of *The House of the Seven Gables* argues that recent attempts to impose a narrowly Freudian psychoanalytic approach upon the work to reduce it to coherence unnecessarily do violence to the concept of "modern psychology" Hawthorne speaks of in his first chapter. Karlow argues for a more literary approach to the science in the work by way of R. D. Laing's model for the structure of the schizophrenic personality. Lisa Steinman examines William Carlos Williams's ambivalent attitude toward science and its products. It is not so much, she argues, that his early poetics produces poems that "more self-consciously than machines reveal human inventiveness" as that "knowledge, language, poems, plants, and men are structurally similar, and their structural essence is best described by analogy to machines or technological products." She proceeds to consider how Einstein provides an image of modern science for Williams. Kenneth Newell considers Pattern, Concrete, and Computer poetry as successive offspring of the idea of the "poem as object"—an idea, we recall, that the Scriblerians long ago derided—and suggests ways that such poetry has a future as a literary activity rather than a pure machine product.

The editors think that the papers in this issue suggest the range and complexity of the questions raised by the relationship between literature and science, as well as point to some answers for our contemporary world.

James M. Heath
Associate Editor

Science and Literature

Theoretical
Approaches

Models for the History of Science and of Literature

John Neubauer

University of Pittsburgh

> Hypotheses are nets; only he who casts will catch.
> Wasn't even America found through a hypothesis?
> . . . The true maker of hypotheses is but an inventor
> to whom the discovered land often darkly presents
> itself prior to the invention, who hovers with his dark
> image above observation and experiment. Only
> through a free comparison, through multiple contact
> and friction with experience does he finally hit upon
> the [right] idea.

THIS statement on the methodology of science in a dialogue by Novalis[1] represents one of the early defenses of
hypotheses in the face of their rejection by Newton. The first
sentence, "Theories are nets; only he who casts will catch," was
adopted by Karl Popper as an epigraph for his *Logik der
Forschung* (1934), a work that was among the first attacks on the
theory and methodology of logical empiricism. (Note, however,
how Popper slants the original meaning by translating "hypotheses" with "theories"!) That Popper, who is by no means a latter-day Romantic, should be able to use a passage from Novalis
is symptomatic of the ways in which philosophers of science
have reinterpreted the making of science and laid the
ground—if only unwittingly—for a far more promising rapprochement between science and literature than anything
which emerged from the dreary debate on the "two cultures."
Surveying these new approaches, I intend to explore their relevance to the historiography of literature.

17

I

Logical empiricism, against which Popper rebelled, is typified by Rudolf Carnap's dictum that philosophy ought to become the "logic of science, i.e., the logical analysis of the concepts, propositions, proofs, [and] theories of science."[2] Empiricism implied that the scientific attitude had to be "objective" and that the mind of the investigator was free from any religious, psychological, metaphysical, or, for that matter, literary preconceptions. Though the revolution in twentieth-century physics shook the epistemological foundation of empiricism, many theoreticians continued to believe that science ought to proceed inductively, from simple observations to ever more complex generalizations.

Popper's title programmatically announces a shift from a Carnapian logic of science to a Popperian logic operating in the *history* of science, based on "norms, by which the scientist is guided when he is engaged in research or in discovery."[3] Popper hopes to construct a theory of scientific methodology, a philosophy of the history of science, that is descriptive of actual scientific practice and yet also normative.

Recent philosophers of science may diverge from Popper, but many share his dislike for the theoretical models of logical empiricism, and some agree that philosophies of science must account for the historical practice of science. Their very attempt to fuse theory and history into a metahistory should be of obvious interest to the warring historians and theoreticians of literature.

Popper's book didn't have any serious impact until its revised and enlarged English edition appeared in 1959, twenty-five years later, under the title *The Logic of Scientific Discovery*. By that time, a considerably larger segment of the scientific and philosophic community was willing to accept Popper's claim that science proceeds not by induction from singular to universal statements but by the invention of hypotheses and the empirical testing of their consequences. The theory nets are cast, as Popper says, "to catch what we call the world: to rationalize, to explain, and to master it. We endeavor to make the mesh ever finer and finer" (*LSD*, p. 59). It is perhaps indicative of Popper's distance from the author of his epigraph that for Novalis the success of fishing lies not in the refinement of webbing technology but in the idiosyncratic art of individual fishermen. As a character in *Die Lehrlinge zu Sais* remarks, "the more haphazardly the daring fisherman's net is woven, the better his catch."[4]

But Popper's differences with the Romantic position go further. The invention of hypotheses becomes a subject matter for the psychology of creativity. Popper is concerned with the scrutiny of hypotheses, and the means used in this process become for him the "demarcation criteria" that distinguish science from myth, religion, literature, and the pseudo-sciences. That search for demarcation is in direct contrast to Romantic visions of a science merged with other fields of culture. For Popper, science is the rational and critical enterprise par excellence, conducted in the spirit of a Platonic Academy. Unfortunately, his disinterest in psychology weakens the descriptive dimension of his model. Demanding that scientists masochistically and cunningly devise ever subtler ways to falsify their theories instead of clinging to them tooth and nail, he exacts a behavior that flies in the face of experience. While popular belief identifies science with indubitability, Popper finds its hallmark in the experimental falsifiability of its statements.

Since scientific theories always extend beyond the sphere of experimental verification, tests can never establish the unquestioned soundness of a theory, only its incorrectness. To emphasize this, Popper added to the introduction of the third German edition of his book a new epigraph from Kant, which admits that even a single untrue consequence will falsify a scientific statement. Hence, the prime value of tests lies in their ability to refute rather than to confirm. A theory is scientific if it can be exposed to falsification by testing. Science progresses, according to the title of another book by Popper, by means of *Conjectures and Refutations,* but the creative conjectures are merely ancillary to the critical process whereby conjectures are scrutinized and refuted.

II

Popper's *Logic of Scientific Discovery* prepared the ground for Thomas Kuhn's *Structure of Scientific Revolutions,*[5] and, for all their differences, Popper and Kuhn agree on such fundamental issues as the denial that science grows by induction and accretion. But Kuhn distinguishes between "extraordinary" and "normal" science, reducing the latter to an essentially puzzle-solving activity "firmly based upon one or more past scientific achievements, achievements that some particular scientific community acknowledges for a time as supplying the foundation for its further practice" (*SSR,* p. 10). According to Kuhn, Ptolemy's *Almagest,* Newton's *Principia* and *Opticks,* and Lyell's *Geology* contain paradigms, because they defined "the legitimate problems and methods of a research field for succeeding generations of practitioners" (*SSR,* p. 10). In the course of normal science the validity of paradigms cannot be questioned, and anomalies must be resolved within their framework. At certain rare moments, however, anomalies multiply and resist coercion, producing a paradigm crisis. New modes of explanations surface, a revolution occurs, and in due time the old paradigm is replaced by a new one. For Kuhn, the critical discourse of Popperian science takes place, then, only during its occasional revolutionary periods, and the emergence of a "normal" and mature science is marked by the abandonment of critical discourse: "Once a field has made that transition, critical discourse recurs only at moments of crisis when the bases of the field are again in jeopardy. Only when they must choose between competing theories do scientists behave like philosophers."[6] In short, tradition and communal authority, not critical discourse, characterize science.

I shall have to restrict myself here to a few observations on the relevance of paradigms to literature.[7] It may be thought that scientific paradigms allow for an integration of the dominant scientific ideas into the intellectual milieu of their age. Kuhn's early book on the *The Copernican Revolution* does not yet use the term, but it suggests an interrelation between science, philosophy, and art by claiming, for instance, that the embodiment of the Aristotelian-Christian-Ptolemaic world view in the *Divine Comedy* delayed the transition to Copernicanism: "when angels become the motive force of epicycles and deferents, the variety of spiritual creatures in God's legion may increase with the complexity of astronomical theory. Astronomy is no longer quite separate from theology. Moving the earth may necessitate moving God's Throne."[8] But Kuhn now thinks that such interrelations typify only "immature" science, for "practitioners of a mature science are effectively insulated from the cultural milieu in which they live their extra-professional lives."[9] Stung by the criticism that his use of paradigms is ambiguous, Kuhn has come to stress their disciplinary dimension and their role in defining the habits of scientific communities. He now distinguishes between broader "disciplinary matrices," which embrace "all the shared commitments of a scientific group," and more restricted "exemplars," which are imitated by a narrower group of scientists.[10] None of these new meanings allow for an interdisciplinary use.

In the final analysis, Kuhn is ambiguous with respect to interdisciplinary integrations of science. While he perceives a great need to bridge the chasm between historians of science and historians of ideas,[11] he seeks to understand scientific growth in terms of the unique professional habits of its practitioners. He believes that his own book denies, "at least by strong implication, that art can readily be distinguished from science by application of the classic dichotomies between, for example, the world of value and the world of fact, the subjective and the objective, or the intuitive and the inductive" (*ET*, p. 340), but he finds the rapprochement between science and the arts "disquieting" and the search for demarcation criteria a necessity (*ET*, p. 341). Of course, Kuhn can no longer rely on Popperian falsifiability as an adequate criterion of separation. Not the rational discussion and testing of ideas, but "the role of competing schools and of incommensurable traditions, of changing standards of value, and of altered modes of perception" (*ET*, p. 340) become for him the hallmark of science.

Thus Kuhn tends to define science as the activity of its practitioners, and his shift of attention from rational discourse to the sociology and psychology of the discoursers has undoubtedly opened new horizons for a comparative study of the sciences and the arts. But many who rush into this new territory tend to overlook Kuhn's view that the very uniqueness of the psychology and sociology of science gives us new criteria of demarcation. Thus efforts to develop a sociology of literature on a Kuhnian basis are often ill conceived and even in contradiction to his intention. I shall give two examples, Hans Robert Jauss's article "Paradigmawechsel in der Literaturwissenschaft"[12] and Grant Webster's recent book *The Republic of Letters*,[13] both of which claim to apply Kuhnian structures.

Both of these studies offer a sociology of literary scholarship instead of a sociology of literary creativity, silently passing over a fundamental imbalance in the analogy between literature and science. As the diagram below indicates, Kuhn is a metacritic who studies the ways in which scientists study nature and interact with each other. What should be the subject matter of Jauss, Webster, and other Kuhnian metacritics of literature? There is a fundamental difference in the artifacts, for art is man-made while nature is not. Unlike the metacritic of science, who has to deal with a fairly homogeneous group of scientists, the metacritic of literature (and all the other arts) has to study the function and behavior of two very different groups, the artists and the literary scholar-critics. The complex interaction between these two groups not only affects their behavior, but subtly modifies also the manner in which art is created in the first place. A metacritic of literature may, of course, focus on any dimension of the triangle between art, the artist, and the scholar-critic, as long as the reader is made aware of the external dimensions. But I would argue that in adopting a Kuhnian approach the literary metacritic should focus first on the changes that occur in literature itself (why and how, for instance, style shifts between the enlightenment and romanticism).

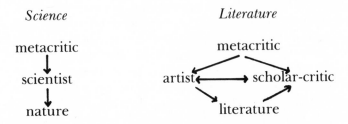

There are other problems as well. Jauss, who has become a major authority on the sociology of literary reception, makes surprisingly little use of the Kuhnian sociology of paradigms. He identifies paradigmatic methods in the history of criticism, the classical, the historicist, and the stylistic or *werkimmanent*. However, he is ultimately concerned with the present paradigm crisis and the nature of the fourth, new paradigm that will eventually emerge from it. For those who read between the lines, it becomes evident that Jauss hopes for the enthroning of a reception theory. Given Jauss's concern about the future, perhaps one should not fault him too much for his sketch of the past. Nevertheless, one ought to note that neither of these paradigms was ever coherent (historicism, for instance, encompasses both positivism and *Geistesgeschichte*) or universally accepted. All three, and some others, competed with each other during the increasing critical pluralism of the last fifty years. The fault lies partly in the crudeness of Jauss's model, but, as we shall see, one can similarly counter to Kuhn that the long stretches of "normal science" represent a constant war of conflicting paradigms.

Webster, who studies the postwar trends in American criticism as a deliberate extension of Kuhn's theory (*RL*, p. 4), is aware of the permanence of paradigmatic conflicts: in his dictionary, the Kuhnian paradigms become "Charters," defined as "a set of literary values which relies on a grant of intellectual authority, is embodied in a document, organizes a critical community, and is limited in time and function, with the corollary that society as a whole can support a variety of critical charters" (*RL*, p. 10). But if the normal condition of criticism is to have a plurality of charters, these can have no coercive force, and the whole Kuhnian distinction between normal and extraordinary science loses its relevance. Similarly, there can be no equivalent to the role of anomalies, adjudication between competing schools of thought, and the notion of progress in science. Webster admits of these differences and even upholds them as signs of his autonomous treatment of the subject, but the asymmetry is so great that the analogy to Kuhnian science becomes an empty gesture and questionable appeal to an outside authority. Whenever he does draw parallels between scientific and critical practices, as for instance in establishing an analogy between critical approaches and scientific subspecialties, he becomes vague and unconvincing: "If one takes as the proper parallel 'physicist/Freudian critic' or 'scientist/critic,' then determining the relationship of scientist to critic is about the same as asking whether knowledge is to be gained by approaching nature as physicist or biologist, or literature as Formalist or Myth Critic; the relationship between the various kinds of science and criticism is about the same" (*RL*, p. 40). But physics and biology are not "incompatible and unrelated" views of nature as, in Webster's opinion, the different schools of criticism are.

Comparative studies of literature and science will have to go different routes and cannot merely rely on Kuhn's theory of paradigms, which has been more widely accepted by nonspecialists than by theorists of science. Kuhn's theory is itself a powerful paradigm for historical change, but it is one among several competing ones, just as the paradigms of science always are. Its value lies not in its correctness but in its ability to stimulate further thought and discussion—although Kuhn himself seems to disparage the confrontation of clashing opinions as a Popperian manner of proceeding.

III

If Kuhn gave new impetus to the sociology of science, Paul Feyerabend is the psychologist of rugged individualism. He radicalizes the Kuhnian revolution by further loosening the rational cohesion of science and strengthening its links to the arts. Feyerabend subtitles his *Against Method* as an *Outline of an Anarchistic Theory of Knowledge,* but in order to avoid the charge of defending terrorism he now prefers to see science as a "Dadaist" enterprise.[14] It is amusing to contemplate that theories of science moved from Novalis to Dada in a mere forty years!

Feyerabend uses Galileo's advocacy of Copernicanism to illustrate his thesis that scientific change is not the product of rational considerations and arguments. As Feyerabend sees it, Galileo's faulty arguments involved deliberate deception and demagoguery, not, as Brecht would have it, to trick the suppressors, but to win the support of fellow scientists and the interested public. Copernicanism and other valuable scientific ideas survived "because prejudice, passion, conceit, errors, sheer pigheadedness . . . opposed the dictates of reason and because these irrational elements were permitted to have their way" (*AM,* p. 155). Generalizing from this case, Feyerabend pleads for ruthlessly opportunistic scientists who adopt a "methodological anarchy" to fit the occasion (*AM,* p. 18). Not only should promising theories continue to be studied in the face of refuting instances (*AM,* pp. 30, 47f., and 77), even outmoded theories should be kept in mind—a powerful argument for studying the history of science. Feyerabend rightly claims that no scientific explanation is ever fully consistent (*AM,* p. 35), that facts are never independent of theory and ideology (*AM,* pp. 30, 41f., and 77), and that scientific ideas often start with an irrelevant activity, such as play, rather than rational considerations and criticism (*AM,* pp. 167 and 176). Hence his ideal is not a Popperian critical discourse but an enterprise in which scientists "proceed in their own way, devising their own task and assembling their own domain of facts" in sovereign disregard for others (*AM,* p. 176). For its greater glory, science ought to borrow and pilfer "from religion, from mythology, from the ideas of incompetents, or the ramblings of madmen" (*AM,* p. 68). No view is too absurd or immoral, no method is indispensable; only universal standards and laws, or "universal ideas such as 'Truth,' 'Reason,' 'Justice,' 'Love' and the behavior they bring along," (*AM*, p. 189) are absolutely opposed by Feyerabend's ideal scientist.

There is surely something disarming about this iconoclastic view of an iconoclastic science. Since Feyerabend's ideas often contain a grain of truth and his rugged individualism is endowed with an aesthetic sensibility, his appeal will reach beyond the Dadaist circle. Yet, his reading distorts the history of science as much as earlier empiricist and positivist theories did. If Feyerabend's view were to become practice, science would join the arts in an exhibitionist show on a Dadaist stage. As Thomas Kuhn says in another context, "there is no scientific avant-garde, and the existence of one would threaten science" (*ET*, p. 350).

It is difficult to criticize a theory that claims to be no system at all, since its author reserves for himself the right to change premises at random and contradict what he said earlier. But some contradictions seem endemic to Feyerabend's thought, foremost among them the simultaneous belief in radical individualism and intersubjective constructs. He admires the fanatics who build their dream castles on an idée fixe, and even the Dadaists, whose only claim to consistency is their radical dedication to deconstruction. Yet, in spite of his belief in anarchistic individual creativity, Feyerabend reaffirms the existence of comprehensive world views. Men of letters will be most interested in Feyerabend's claim that archaic Greek culture was unified by the elemental underlying principles of additiveness and paratactic grammar. Taking a Whorffian view of language and a variation on *Zeitgeist* and paradigms, Feyerabend postulates that a temporally persistent world view welded together that culture: if we compare the elements of archaic art with the literary style, the sentence construction, the grammar, and the ideology of the age, we discover the underlying forces informing "perception, thought, argument" and limiting the roaming imagination (*AM*, p. 232). The unique core and constructive principle of archaic Greek culture is embedded in every fact or concept of that cultural cosmos (*AM*, p. 269).

The coherence and autonomy of archaic Greek culture becomes for Feyerabend a feature of all cultures, even of our own pluralistic and fragmented one. Cultural systems, like Whorffian languages, are to him so autonomous that one needs a Kuhnian revolution to pass from one to another. In Feyerabend's Dadaist dream, the coherent cultural universes sprout from total creative anarchy.

IV

Kuhn and Feyerabend have effectively demolished a number of rationalist assumptions about the history of science, but their larger historical units seem too impervious to time. Two post-Kuhnian rational models for scientific change by Imre Lakatos and Larry Laudan are more flexible.

Like Feyerabend, Lakatos holds that falsification is seldom conclusive and does not automatically dispose of theories: "It is not that we propose a theory and Nature may shout *no,* rather, we propose a maze of theories and Nature may shout *inconsistent*" (*CGK*, p. 130). Accordingly, Lakatos shifts his attention from the momentary shape of theories to their long-range response to empirical observations and internal inconsistencies: "It is a succession of theories and not one given theory which is appraised as scientific or pseudo-scientific. But the members of such series or theories are usually connected by a remarkable continuity which welds them into research programmes" (*CGK*, p. 132). Scientific change emerges on this account from the constant friction between competing research programs.

By identifying with Kuhnian normal science a competition of interacting research programs, Lakatos argues for the coexistence of widely different scientific theories and methodologies, and he broadens the range of scientific attitudes, to account for rationality as well as psychological and sociological forces. While he wishes to regain ground for rational explanations, he argues that fledgling research programs ought to be protected and nurtured even if they do not as yet seem reasonable, and he acknowledges that a certain amount of Feyerabendian pigheadedness is inevitable. But Lakatos continues to believe that the forces moving a mature science are internal and different from other forces of change, and thus he has little interest in extrascientific ideas and beliefs.

In contrast to Lakatos and others, Laudan sees only a quantitative difference between science and other intellectual disciplines: though the rate of progress is faster in science, its methods and problems are not unique.[15] Laudan defines science as a problem-solving activity which differs from a Kuhnian puzzle solving by being basically rational and progressive. With Feyerabend, Laudan agrees that extrascientific ideas, beliefs, and world views contribute to the development of science, though he singles out rational choices as the ones leading to progress (*PP,* p. 125). With Lakatos, Laudan agrees that the "perennial co-existence of conflicting traditions of research" makes Kuhn's focus on the revolutionary epochs misleading (*PP*, p. 136) and that long-range development and effectiveness determine the value of scientific theories. However, while Lakatos's research programs are insulated, Laudan's research traditions are embedded in world views and interact with philosophy, theology, and other disciplines. They are so flexible that even their "hard core" may change (*PP*, p. 99). Thus the history of science becomes, for Laudan, a species of intellectual history, where rational explanations have priority over psychological and sociological ones.

V

If we take these and other recent theories of science seriously, we may end up with more questions than answers—and with certainly more issues than this paper can accommodate. I should like to focus therefore on two questions that are of prime importance to literary scholars:

1. Do these theories allow a correlation between the science and the literature of a given historical moment?

2. To what extent can the structural features of these models be applied to the history of literature and the arts?

To the first question the theories discussed offer a variety of answers, ranging from Popper's demarcation criteria to Laudan's centrality of intellectual history and Feyerabend's unified cultures. As far as I can see, none of these theorists has suggested or attempted to demonstrate the existence of correlations between the two fields on sociological grounds, comparing the motivation and behavior of scientists and artists at a certain moment of history. On the contrary, Kuhn, whose approach is most strongly sociological, wants to distinguish the two groups precisely on the basis of the unique institutional aspects of scientific training and work. Feyerabend and Laudan believe in structural, thematic, and ideational connections between literature and science, but they hardly give any concrete examples for the ways in which these are produced. *Geistesgeschichte* and the history of ideas have, it is true, offered us many instances, but almost all of them lead from science to literature and all but none in the other direction. Furthermore, the power of the arguments is usually debilitated by an all too facile use of the concept of "influence." Those who attempt to skirt it often fall back on the equally questionable notion of a *Zeitgeist*—

Feyerabend being no exception. Gerald Holton's careful approach to the issue in terms of the "thematic" patterns in science is considerably more promising.[16] However, even Holton lapses on occasion into fanciful speculations, for instance in relating the modern scientific interest in radioactive decay and fission to the disintegration of artistic form.[17] There is, after all, as much interest in nuclear fusion as there is in fission.

In principle, Laudan's view that the history of science is a species of intellectual history seems to provide the most accommodating framework for an interdisciplinary study of the sciences and the arts. But even this is fraught with problems. For Laudan, the typical nonscientific elements in a world view belong to philosophy or theology, disciplines that strive for rational discourse. The arts use modes of discourse that may incorporate varying degrees of reason and may even possess a logic of their own, but they should not be judged solely by the criteria of rationality that Lakatos or Laudan apply to science. To be sure, inasmuch as the arts incorporate ideas they partake in their intellectual milieu, and studies sensitive to the artistic context may identify the ideas in a writer's world view. By so doing one still subsumes literature under the general category of expository prose, and brackets the features of form and style, which, after all, distinguish literature. If we agree that science deals with concepts and literature with concepts as well as forms, we ought to give more attention in the future to the correlation between conceptual and stylistic changes.

This leads to my second question, to what extent the models of scientific change are applicable to the changes in style and form. Dissatisfied with a mere correlation between the period concepts in literature and science, we ought to search for analogies between the modes of change in the two realms. Recent theories of science make no actual comparisons, though they establish models for conceptual changes in science that are not unlike the stylistic and formal changes in literature. In the remainder of this paper I should like to discuss the possible rapprochement between these two modes of change by reconsidering three interrelated and generally accepted views on the history of the arts and the sciences. These may be stated as follows:

1. Artistic forms of the past have vitality and presence, while older scientific theories are dead.

2. The arts merely shift fashions of style, while the sciences genuinely progress.

3. The arts normally accommodate a number of competing styles, while in the sciences incompatible theories can coexist for relatively short periods only.

VI

Let me illustrate these views with representative statements and indicate why they have become questionable. James Ackerman, an art historian, remarks that "our understanding of works of art is not dependent on a knowledge of their historical position"; primitive artifacts "are as valid as the most sophisticated products of highly developed civilizations"; "for the artist of any period, what was produced thousands of years before may be as vital a stimulus as the products of the immediate past."[18] Thomas Kuhn's succinct statement may be read as a complement: "unlike art, science destroys its past" (*ET*, p. 345); "neither out-of-date theories nor even the original formulations of current theory are of much concern to practitioners" of science (*ET*, p. 347). But these are overstatements. Though older works of art may provide inspiration today, they suffer from the ravages of time. The *Divine Comedy*, especially the *Paradiso*, is barely accessible, for instance, without the historical knowledge provided by annotations; even if we possess the requisite erudition, a genuine understanding asks for a "willing suspension" of our own, modern perception of the world. How deep can our understanding of the *Divine Comedy* be without some empathy with Dante's religious inspiration? Theories of reception may often be crude and unsatisfactory, but they are prompted by the surely proper diagnosis that the classics in the arts do not live on as canonized eternal verities; they survive because their richness allows later ages a reinterpretation from their own experiential horizon. How different the surviving meaning can be from the originally intended one may be seen in our preference for the *Inferno* to the *Paradiso*. Scholarly reconstruction of a historical meaning can only replace part of the inevitable loss suffered.

If, on the one hand, the continued vitality and presence of the literary classics depend on ever-shifting perspectives and reinterpretations,[19] it has, on the other hand, been acknowledged by some recent theoreticians that past science has more than historical interest. Feyerabend, Holton, and others correctly observe that outmoded scientific theories never die completely and often experience spectacular resurrections—if only in a changed shape. The atomism of Democritus came to new life in the eighteenth century. Newton's corpuscular theory of light was soundly defeated in the early nineteenth century, only to have a spectacular comeback a hundred years later. Scientific concepts have no objective existence; they are creative inventions that disappear once a theory is falsified but return once new observations favor a former mode of explanation over a recent one. Indeed, there seem to be a few basic ideas and methods that get constantly reinterpreted and thus persist in time.

Historical consciousness is operative, then, in the life of science as well as in that of literature. But what is the form of that history? Do accumulation and progression not separate science from other subjects? The traditional answer echoes in Ackerman's words: "it is improper to speak of the evolution of art in terms of progress except in the limited sense that a particular technique or skill may be systematically improved."[20] Scientific theories may become outdated, but since "no mode of artistic representation can be shown to be right or wrong, there is no parallel to Copernicus' improvement of the Ptolemaic representation of the planetary system."[21] When Kuhn poses the same question in the last chapter of *Structure of Scientific Revolutions,* he seems to have a straight answer: the gains outweigh the losses in revolutions, while during normal science the puzzle-solving ability is cumulative, so that the "successive stages in that developmental process are marked by an increase in articulation and specialization" (*SSR,* p. 171)—a view that corresponds to Popper's metaphoric refinement of fishing nets. Upon closer inspection, Kuhn is equivocating however. He believes that "progress seems both obvious and assured" (*SSR,* p. 162) because normal science "is an immensely efficient instrument for solving problems or puzzles that its paradigms define" (*SSR,* p. 165). For a careful reader, this means that progress seems "obvious and assured" only as long as we accept the premises of the paradigm and the tasks they define; once we take up another frame of reference, once we go through a "Gestalt switch," progress may turn out to be a mirage for having occurred only in the limited area of puzzle solving. Indeed, at times Kuhn suggests that progress in normal science is predicated on the professional organization of scientists, and only "the unparalleled insulation of mature scientific communities from the demands of the laity" (*SSR,* p. 163) leads to that universally accepted single set of standards which is the precondition of progress. Hence, according to Kuhn, "part of the answer to the problem of progress lies simply in the eye of the beholder. Scientific progress is not different in kind from progress in other fields, but the absence at most times of competing schools that question each other's aims and standards makes the progress of a normal-scientific community far easier to see" (*SSR*, p. 162). As far as scientific revolutions are concerned, their histories are written, according to Kuhn, by the camp that won; hence their outcome could not be anything less than progress (*SSR*, p. 165). Since scientific history is written by the vanquishers, might, i.e., the authority of the scientific community, does make right in science (*SSR*, p. 166).

Thus, Kuhn comes very close to saying that progress in science is merely decreed by a group of experts (*SSR*, p. 169), though he refrains from asserting this categorically, and Webster is wrong in imputing to Kuhn the notion that "science as a whole does not progress" (*RL*, p. 48). Kuhn does place, however, severe limitations on the traditional notion of scientific progress by asserting (1) that science is not cumulative, since revolutions bring losses as well as gains (*SSR*, pp. 166 and 168); (2) that scientific growth has no teleology, for it is impossible to say toward what goal it is progressing (*SSR*, pp. 169f.); and (3) that science does not represent objective truth (*SSR*, p. 169). It is not surprising, then, that Kuhn should differentiate between the arts and the sciences on sociological grounds: "to say with pride, as both artists and scientists do, that science is cumulative, art is not, is to mistake the developmental pattern in both fields. Nevertheless, that often repeated generalization does express . . . the radically different value placed upon innovation for innovation's sake by scientists and artists" (*ET*, p. 350). This suggests that one may identify the differences between the arts and the sciences by studying how the professional education of scientists forges an essentially conservative temperament and how artists, on the other hand, are taught to prize "innovation for innovation's sake." It looks as if the premium placed on innovation prevented the arts from progressing.

The position seems somehow fundamentally wrong, but at this point it may suffice perhaps to point out the weakness of a sociological approach that defines modes of creativity in terms of institutions and social behavior. With all due respect to the sociology of the professions, I have to agree with those post-Kuhnian theoreticians who deny that a demarcation of science on sociological grounds is possible. To say that science is what scientists practice, and art what artists do, and to define the differences between these fields in terms of the tribal behavior of their practitioners raises the question of how such different tribes came into being in the first place. The circularity of such an approach is evident. My argument is not directed against Kuhn alone. It has become fashionable for humanists and social scientists to talk about science as just another "mode of discourse," propelled by its rhetoric and by the social organization of its practitioners, being, ultimately, a nonreferential, constructed reality comparable to the arts. This view belittles science's ability to manipulate nature and asserts that science is defined by its unique authority relation, i.e., by the fact that scientific statements must be certified by the "discourse community" that has assumed the guardianship of science. No doubt, the scientific community has its own quaint rituals, in which rationality is but one among many voices. But to suggest that our indubitable technological control over nature is merely a result of the peculiar authority relation within the scientific "discourse community" is tantamount to saying that scientific authority has magical powers over nature and summons its demons in the manner of Goethe's sorcerer's apprentice. The voice of nature may be more elusive than previous generations have thought, but surely, it speaks as loudly as the scientific establishment in giving guidance to long-range developments in science.

This should not be taken as a naive credo in progress and science. Like many others, I am deeply divided on the issue; I find it impossible to deny that great progress has been achieved in the interpretation and manipulation of nature, yet I find corresponding losses in the psychological and sociological domain and vacillate in drawing a balance. While our narrowly technical and manipulative problem-solving ability gradually increases, we seem to be creating new problems in earlier unproblematic areas. However we think of these changes, we must admit that they have so profoundly reshaped our world that the arts cannot escape their impact. To a large extent, changes in the arts are predicated today on changes brought about by science and technology. On their technical side, the arts evidently progress. Musicians can employ a wider range of sounds, painters and sculptors can use new materials and tools, the theater can be equipped with a more sophisticated stagecraft, and language places a richer vocabulary at the disposal of poets. The sophistication is not limited to material-technical means, for it extends over narrative techniques and voices, the uses of time, or complex modes of intertextuality—to mention only a few examples. Such an enlarged repertory of means is, of course, no guarantee for progress in a deeper sense: the limited stage of Aeschylus may be superior to technically and structurally much more sophisticated ones. Yet richness is an aesthetic category as well. Inasmuch as the arts incorporate improved technology, a more comprehensive understanding of the physical world, or more complex artistic structures, they partake, if only in a limited way, in progress. The lack of a broader and deeper progress is often due to a concentration on mere technique or detail which may impoverish art and may lead to the disappearance of already highly developed forms. The *Divine Comedy* is, in its own way, no less complex than Joyce's *Ulysses*, but Joyce is rich with more items that constitute our world.

Much of this holds for the sciences as well, and the differences may only be relative. The Ptolemaic description of planetary motion with deferents and epicycles was an immensely sophisticated explanation that disappeared with the acceptance of the Copernican system. Virtually all the theoreticians of science agree today that such changes always involve losses in knowledge (*SSR*, pp. 166 and 168; *PP*, p. 148) and the gain cannot simply be taken as another step toward some objective body of truth (*PP*, p. 123). The progress in scientific problem solving has been accompanied by increasing uncertainty about its epistemological foundations; the confident belief in science as a pursuit of truth has given way to the uneasy admission that the expansion of knowledge has made its limits more evident and its foundations more obscure. The weakened notion of scientific progress, which no longer entails cumulative growth, teleology, and approach toward an objective truth, may provide a sufficient basis for a comparative study of the arts and the sciences. We should not force that analogy by denying all progress to science.

The notion of progress is intimately linked up with my final question, whether art is pluralistic and science unified. Ackerman will, once more, illustrate the traditional view: the exhaustion of Mannerist art led to a venomous fight between the Classicists, Rubens, and Naturalism, which was "still smoldering 200 years later and died down not in consequence of a victory by one camp, but by a shift of the focus of interest to other problems."[22] In contrast, the controversy between the heliocentric and geocentric systems, which broke out about the same time, was bound to be resolved in a definitive manner in favor of one side. Ackerman fails to add that, since relativity theory has proclaimed that we have no means to determine what bodies, if any, are at absolute rest, the notion of a center has lost its traditional meaning. The example oversimplifies scientific change and controversy. Kuhn, who believes that the revolutionary differences between scientists are definitely resolved during normal science, subscribes to a similar view and adheres to the traditional distinction between the sciences and the arts: "just because the success of one artistic tradition does not render another wrong or mistaken, art can support, far more readily than science, a number of simultaneous incompatible traditions or schools. For the same reason, when traditions do change, the accompanying controversies are usually resolved far more rapidly in science than in art" (*ET,* p. 348).

But this contrast, predicated on the Kuhnian notion of a homogeneous normal science with universally accepted paradigms, is unconvincing.[23] As Laudan puts it, "virtually every major period in the history of science is characterized . . . by the co-existence of numerous competing paradigms" (*PP,* p. 74; see also 134ff.). While such battles do get resolved, they often flare up at a later date. The alternating acceptance and rejection of the corpuscular theory of light, of atomism, or of the notion of a continental drift demonstrates that scientific issues are never conclusively settled. Kuhn attributes the standards of science to a social group rather than nature, but he continues to believe that these standards are strictly enforced and universally held. It is the great merit of the recent theories of science to have recognized that inconsistencies within theories and unresolved disputes between rival paradigms are no mere revolutionary irregularities but the normal condition of science. Newtonian science, for example, had a formative impact on eighteenth-century research, but it meant radically different things to different people, depending on the texts they regarded as authoritative and the idiosyncratic reading they gave to them. Its philosophical foundations and implications continued to be questioned, so that the theory and the methodology of the age remained eclectic. "A scientist can often be working alternately in two different, and even mutually inconsistent, research traditions" (*PP,* p. 110).

VII

I hope it will be evident, even without my sketching out the details, that this new picture of science is relevant to the historiography of literature not because it offers a radically new model, but in confirming, from quite unexpected quarters, what thoughtful literary scholars have been suggesting for some time. It has become evident that the historicist model of *Geistesgeschichte,* with its monolithic periods dominated by a Baroque, a Renaissance, a Classicist, or a Romantic *Zeitgeist,* is as inadequate for the comprehension of the historical profusion and interaction of styles and forms as the Kuhnian paradigms are for the history of science. The longer historical durations of artistic styles and movements are characterized by the kind of inner shifts and changes that are typical of research programs or traditions. Their effectiveness and articulateness increases, climaxes, and declines not in solitary splendor but in constant interaction with other, coexistent movements and styles. And as scientific theories are never quite pure and consistent distillations of a paradigm, so, too, no period, author, or literary work is a pure embodiment of a style. The seventeenth century blends Baroque with Classicism and Mannerism; the classical works of Goethe incorporate Enlightenment, *Sturm und Drang,* and Romantic elements; the great works of nineteenth-century Realism are now Romantic, now Symbolist. Such a dissolution of cohesive units may seem to open the door for chaos, for a nominalist image of literary history with no larger ordering principles. But we are more than compensated for the elimination of period labels by gaining diachronic strands of styles, concepts, and approaches which survive over longer periods of history by adjusting to the external forces of society, ideology, and competing traditions, on the one hand, and the internal forces emerging from the dynamics of movement, on the other. The eventual disappearance of such strands corresponds to the gradual disappearance of a research tradition. Such *Stilwandlungen* do not respond to observed anomalies, but neither do they occur, in my opinion, because of the whim or the "will to power" of some young Turks, as Webster seems to believe. To be sure, such personal and social motives do matter. But the inability of an old style to give articulation to new problems, whether these are intellectual, social, or related to form and style, is of prime importance. While the relative weight of extrinsic and intrinsic forces may vary from case to case, as a rule both will be present, representing just two sides of the same coin. Styles and forms respond to new historical situations as much as to certain unresolved formal problems. The poetic language of Eliot, for example, emerges from certain Symbolist trends but is, at the same time, a genuine image of extraliterary cultural forces at work.

A passage in Claudio Guillén's essay "Second Thoughts on Literary Periods" proposes a model uncannily similar to the ones historians applied to science:

> My hypothesis is that a section of historical time . . . should not be monistically understood as an undivided entity, a bloc, a unit, but as a plural number or cluster of temporal processes, "currents," "durations," rhythms or sequences—flowing . . . simultaneously and side by side.[24]

There exists, then, a surprising unanimity about the nature of time and historical change. In the exploration of that simultaneous flow side by side lies perhaps the greatest promise for future comparatist studies in literature and science.

1. Novalis, *Schriften*, ed. Paul Kluckhohn and Richard Samuel, 2d ed. (Stuttgart: Kohlhammer, 1960–), 2:668f. All translations mine unless otherwise indicated.

2. Rudolf Carnap, "On the Character of Philosophic Problems," in Richard Rorty, ed., *The Linguistic Turn: Recent Essays in Philosophical Method* (Chicago: University of Chicago Press, 1967), pp. 54f.

3. Karl R. Popper, *The Logic of Scientific Discovery* (New York: Harper Torchbook, 1968), p. 50. Further references to this book will be made in the text, cited as *LSD*.

4. Novalis, *Schriften*, 1:98.

5. Thomas Kuhn, *Structure of Scientific Revolutions* (Chicago: University of Chicago Press, 1962). Further references to this book will be made in the text, cited as *SSR*.

6. Thomas Kuhn, "Logic of Discovery or Psychology of Research," in *Criticism and the Growth of Knowledge*, ed. Imre Lakatos and Alan Musgrave (London: Cambridge University Press, 1970), pp. 6f. Further references to this book will be made in the text, cited as *CGK*.

7. A critical discussion of Kuhn's theory and a response by him is contained in the essays in *Criticism and the Growth of Knowledge*.

8. Thomas Kuhn, *The Copernican Revolution* (Cambridge, Mass.: Harvard University Press, 1957), p. 114.

9. Thomas Kuhn, "History of Science," in *International Encyclopedia of the Social Sciences* (New York: Macmillan, 1968–79), p. 81.

10. Thomas Kuhn, *The Essential Tension: Selected Studies in Scientific Tradition and Change* (Chicago: University of Chicago Press, 1977), pp. 293ff. Further references to this book will be made in the text, cited as *ET*. See also Kuhn's Postscript to the second edition of *The Structure of Scientific Revolutions* (1970).

11. Kuhn, *International Encyclopedia of the Social Sciences*, p. 78.

12. Hans Robert Jauss, "Paradigmawechsel in der Literaturwissenschaft," *Linguistische Berichte* 1 (1969): 44–56.

13. Grant Webster, *The Republic of Letters: A History of Postwar American Literary Opinion* (Baltimore, Md.: Johns Hopkins University Press, 1979). All further references to this book will be made in the text, cited as *RL.*

14. Paul Feyerabend, *Against Method: Outline of an Anachronistic Theory of Knowledge* (London: Verso, 1978), pp. 21, 32, and 189. Further references to this book will be made in the text, cited as *AM.*

15. Larry Laudan, *Progress and Its Problems: Towards a Theory of Scientific Growth* (Berkeley, Calif.: University of California Press, 1977). References to this book will be made in the text, cited as *PP.*

16. Gerald Holton, *The Thematic Origins of Scientific Thought* (Cambridge, Mass.: Harvard University Press, 1973).

17. Ibid., p. 95.

18. James Ackerman, "The Demise of the Avant Garde: Notes on the Sociology of Recent American Art," *Comparative Studies in Society and History* 11 (1969): 372.

19. The appeal of older art will, of course, vary from one art form to another. In general, the fine arts and music have a more intense immediacy.

20. Ackerman, "Demise of the Avant Garde," p. 372.

21. Ibid., p. 373.

22. Ibid.

23. The arguments against Kuhn may recall Michel Foucault's attack on "total history," where all phenomena of an epoch are assembled around a single center, "a principle, a meaning, a spirit, a world-view, an overall shape." See *The Archeology of Knowledge*, trans. A.M. Sheridan Smith (New York: Harper, 1972), p. 10. Brief comments must suffice here. Kuhnian paradigms may be fitted into a Hegelian view of history inasmuch as they dominate longer periods and are separated from each other by qualitative revolutions, but they are limited to science, based on sociology, and not moving toward any teleological goal. All in all, it would be a mistake to draw a parallel between the breaking up of the Kuhnian periods of normal science and Foucault's attempt to "disperse" Hegelian history. On the one hand, Kuhn does not link paradigms to a *Zeitgeist;* as we have seen, he regards them as successful models, whose guidance is enforced by the scientific community. On the other hand, Foucault, in the end, curiously resuscitates a model of larger units, called *epistemes*, separated by basic divisions, called "ruptures" or "discontinuities." Recent models of conflicting scientific traditions or programs are therefore incompatible with Foucault's approach. There is, indeed, a growing rift between French and Anglo-American historiographies of science, and it is not obvious to me that Foucault's greater reputation and authority among historians of literature is justified.

24. Claudio Guillén, *Literature as System: Essays toward the Theory of Literary History* (Princeton, N.J.: Princeton University Press, 1971), p. 464.

Epistemological Historicism and the Arts and Sciences

James M. Curtis

University of Missouri–Columbia

I N his thoughtful book *Literary Sociology and Practical Criticism,* Jeffrey Sammons states:

> No enterprise that seeks to put one area of experience into relation with another can avoid some postulation of analogous relationships, for no matter how radically the interpenetration of literature and society may be seen, it is logically impossible to assert that they are congruent and coextensive.[1]

But, a few pages later, Sammons warns, "Almost anything can be amalgamated by the analogical method."[2] In this essay, the tension between these two statements will generate a brief critique of Marxism-Leninism as a holistic theory on the grounds of internal inconsistency, and propose a new one, which employs a method I will call epistemological historicism.

Lenin's *Materialism and Empirio-Criticism* (1907) constitutes an essential text for an epistemological analysis of Marxism-Leninism. In it we find, among Lenin's many fierce attacks on rival interpretations of Marx, the following denunciation of a Russian Marxist who had suggested that recent developments in science had made some of Engels's comments about Newtonian space and time seem dated:

> To tear off Engels' doctrine about the objective reality of time and space from his doctrine about the transformation of "things in themselves" into "things for us," from the recognition of an objective and absolute truth [which is] precisely the objective reality given to us in sensation—from his recognition of objective regularities—this is to turn a holistic philosophy into a crumb.[3]

Here and elsewhere, Lenin vehemently defends the validity of Newtonian physics against all comers, especially scientists. In a most indicative statement Lenin explicitly identifies perception with Newtonian time and space: "Our 'experience' and our cognition are more and more becoming adapted to *objective* space and time, more and more correctly and deeply *reflecting* them."[4]

These two statements suggest, and a more detailed treatment of Lenin's writings would show conclusively, that Lenin took Newtonian space and time as a metaphor for Marxism-Leninism, since he wished to attribute to his philosophy the qualities of objectivity, homogeneity, and absolutism that characterized Newton's physical principles.[5] This analogy enabled him to use the much-prized adjective *objective*, and the suprapersonal qualities of space and time created an implicit disavowal of psychological factors in history.

However, the use of objective space and time as an analogy for a theory of historical development creates some severe epistemological problems, for what the Newtonian universe did not do, by definition, was change. In discussing what he calls the implicit elimination of time in classical physics, Milič Čapek concludes that for Newtonian physics, "the lapse of time is a mere accident: matter and its laws are the same whether we consider them within cosmic aeons or within excessively minute intervals of time."[6] While showing the presence of an internal contradiction, of a belief in historical change as well as a denial of the possibility of historical change, would involve an extensive analysis, one can briefly show how the implications of this contradiction appear in the practice of several Marxist critics.

Newtonian physics attained its highest prestige and most complete acceptance in the nineteenth century, which is also the period of literature that most interests Marxist critics such as Lukács, and with which they have had the greatest success. The Newtonian universe, with its rigid distinction between the framework of objective space and the matter which it contains, becomes in Marxist criticism an emphasis on the content of the work. If the structure is everywhere the same, one can of course ignore it. When even the undoubtedly brilliant Lucien Goldmann discusses "form," his concept of form in fact closely resembles what non-Marxist critics would call "content."[7]

The Michelson-Morley experiment, which disproved the ether theories and thus by implication Newtonian homogeneous space, took place in 1887, and this date may serve to

mark the end of the period in which Marxist critics feel com-
fortable. Marxism has consistently attacked modern art and
modern science together; as a case in point, Sammons cites
Ernst Bloch's characterization of jazz as "American filth" and
Theodor Adorno's opinion that the saxophone is an inferior
musical instrument.[8] One cannot refute these perceptions directly, but one *can* refer them to their social origins; Sammons
inquires:

> I wonder whether Marxist literary criticism, in the largest historical
> sense, is not part of the whole effort of the Western intelligentsia in
> the first half of this century to seek salvation from the apparent
> disintegration of traditional civilization in literary culture.[9]

A psychohistorical study of the prominent Marxist critics of the
twentieth century, such as Lukács, Goldmann, Adorno, and
Bloch, might well refer their conservative artistic and intellectual tastes to their social milieux, and might well show an unconscious need to retain the values of the elitist, highly verbal
Central European culture that gave them such high status.

Such an analysis would proceed from what I take as an essential assumption of historicism: any intellectual theory or social
phenomenon may be interpreted with regard to something
other than itself. And it is just this which Lenin denies when, in
State and Revolution (1917), he assails everyone who dared to
interpret or modify Marx. In turn, contemporary Marxists
would not admit the validity of any interpretation of Lenin's
own life and work except on his own terms. Thus, Marxism is a
philosophy of history that denies its own historicity.

I do not believe that an attempt to achieve a holistic understanding of the interrelationships between the arts and the sciences, an attempt that has great appeal in a world of dizzying
complexity, is inherently futile and reductive. Rather, it is the
analogy with *Newtonian* science that has a reductive effect; while
that analogy may offer some suggestive features with regard to
the art of the nineteenth century, it can only condemn the arts
of the twentieth century, the age of Einsteinian physics. Therefore, I wish to set forth here the possibility of an analogy with
Einsteinian physics, one that assumes a more completely assimilated historicism than that in Marxism.

"History, if viewed as a repository for more than anecdote or
chronology, could produce a decisive transformation in the image of science by which we are now possessed."[10] Thus begins

the most influential book on the philosophy of science in recent times, Thomas S. Kuhn's *The Structure of Scientific Revolutions.* Kuhn's historicism takes the form of a denial that science proceeds by arriving at ever more accurate descriptions of the external world; instead of this linear conception of the history of science, he develops a theory of science as discontinuous. His now famous term *paradigm* refers to an intellectual structure that predominates in a given period and that another paradigm may replace, as Einsteinian physics has replaced Newtonian physics. Kuhn also denies that reasoning alone can bring about what he calls a "gestalt switch," after which a scientist perceives the world in a different way. Logic does not necessarily play a role in this: "Something must make at least a few scientists feel that the new proposal is on the right track, and sometimes it is only personal and inarticulate aesthetic considerations that can do that."[11]

Kuhn's suggestion that "aesthetic considerations" may play a key role in the development of science offers a hint that historicism may help us to understand the interrelations between the arts and sciences, and Harold Brown's *Perception, Theory, and Commitment* clarifies the matter. After arguing forcefully for paradigms as constitutive of scientific research, Brown concludes:

> Thus scientific knowledge in any era is what the scientists take as such, and the scientific knowledge of one era may be rejected as error in the next. But the rejection of previously accepted claims will itself be made on the basis of the currently accepted views, which are themselves fallible.[12]

To reject previous scientific paradigms with an awareness that one's own paradigm may be similarly rejected in time is to assimilate into one's research a historical self-consciousness. Brown cites a striking example of the insidious results of a lack of such historical self-consciousness in the writings of an astronomer whose own recent work had been invalidated by the use of new techniques, yet who continued to believe that little had changed, or would change. He comments:

> Even a cursory study of twentieth century science makes it extremely difficult to understand such serene confidence, and it is equally difficult to see how science can benefit from perpetuating the myth that it is the "established results," rather than the ongoing research, that is the lifeblood of science.[13]

If we deny that the purpose of science is "to get the right answers," we must then say something like "the purpose of science is science," which sounds very consistent with the modernist principle that "the purpose of art is art."

One thus notes a consistency between the conceptions of art and science in the nineteenth century, and between the conceptions of art and science in the twentieth century. In the nineteenth century, scientists generally thought of themselves as describing an external reality, and artists generally thought of themselves as dealing with a social reality. Moreover, both of these realities have a strongly visual nature. Čapek cites, for instance,

> the precept which John Tyndall recommended in his Liverpool address to the physicists of the Victorian era as a reliable criterion of satisfactory scientific theory: "Ask your imagination if it will accept it," i.e., ask yourself if you are able to draw a mental picture of the phenomenon in question; reject it if no visual diagram, no mechanical model can be constructed. This demand hardly varied from the seventeenth to the nineteenth century; Tyndall's recommendation is basically the same as that of Descartes and Huygens.[14]

In literature, one can cite the well-known epigraph to chapter 13 of volume 1 of Stendhal's *The Red and the Black:* "A novel is a mirror which one takes for a walk along a road."[15] Even today, critics say that a novel "reflects" the society of its time, the views of the author, or whatever. In both cases, these visual metaphors bespeak a tendency to identify art and literature with some external reality.

In the twentieth century, however, it has become increasingly difficult to justify visual models. This is most obvious in abstract painting, of course, but much of modern poetry has no clear referent either. Likewise, in science, no one has ever seen an electron, and no one ever will, but that does not mean that scientists do not believe in the existence of electrons.

A paradigm for explaining the concomitant demise of the emphasis on visualization and the rise of historicism appears in Gottlob Frege's essay "On Sense and Reference" (1892). Just at the time when scientists were realizing that they could not identify space with Euclidean geometry, Frege suggested that "identity (in the mathematical sense) demands examination through questions which are connected with it and which are not easily answered" (p. 43).[16] Accordingly, he resolved propositions into "sense" (*Sinn*) and "reference" (*Bedeutung*). While "reference" refers to the information about the world which the proposition gives (that is, its relationship to an external reality), "sense" refers to its internal coherence: "It may perhaps be granted that every grammatically well-formed expression representing a proper name always has a sense" (p. 58). Frege noted, however—and this is a key to his analysis—that one can easily compose grammatically well-formed expressions which have no reference, i.e., give no knowledge about the external world: "The words 'the celestial body most distant from the Earth' have a sense, but it is very doubtful if they have a reference" (p. 58). Frege was thus arguing that the sense and the reference of a proposition (or a theory) are not necessarily identical to each other, and that careful analysis will distinguish them. After developing the argument in this manner in several pages, Frege comes to a crucial passage:

> The sentence "Odysseus was set ashore at Ithaca while sound asleep" obviously has a sense. But since it is doubtful whether the name "Odysseus" occurring therein has a reference, it is also doubtful whether the whole sentence has one. [P. 62]

Since, for Frege, the truth value of a proposition corresponds to its reference, and since art has no truth value (that is, it cannot be proved true or false), one can consider a work of art a proposition which has sense, but no reference.

> In hearing an epic poem, for instance, apart from the euphony of the language we are interested only in the sense of the sentences and the images and the feelings thereby aroused. The question of truth would cause us to abandon aesthetic delight for an attitude of scientific investigation. Hence it is a matter of no concern to us, as long as we accept the poem as a work of art. [P. 63]

Frege, a mathematician and logician, wrote in the last years of French Symbolism, and his use of examples from Homer implies that his method may apply to both the arts and the sciences.

To use the method of epistemological historicism means to assume that both scientific theories and works of art have a sense as well as a reference, and to understand that while historical change may invalidate the reference, it will not invalidate the sense. Traditionally, people have believed that art lasted longer than science, since science could be invalidated by new discoveries. (By way of compensation, science could affect art—as in Newton's effect on English poetry—but art has rarely affected science.) But to believe this is to make an identity between sense and reference, or between paradigm and subject matter. This belief implies that once a scientific theory no longer describes the real world accurately, it loses all interest for us. However, one can always distinguish between the ostensible subject of a scientific theory, and the paradigm which generates it, and to do so makes historical understanding possible. To distinguish the paradigm from the subject matter—an epistemological operation—and then to refer that paradigm to the social process in which it arose, is the essential procedure of epistemological historicism. The use of such a procedure retains a certain historical meaning for any major paradigm from any period of history.

Consider, for example, Kuhn's comments on what he calls "the much-maligned phlogiston theory," the theory that prevailed in eighteenth-century chemistry before the understanding of the properties of oxygen.

> It explained why bodies burned—they were rich in phlogiston—and why metals had so many more properties in common than did their ores. The metals were all compounded from different elementary earths combined with phlogiston, and the latter, common to all metals, produced common properties.[17]

A description of the phlogiston theory not simply as a mass of errors but as a consistent paradigm that solved certain research problems makes it possible for us to understand those who believed in it not simply as stupid or unenlightened but as serious scientists who had reasons for their belief. Moreover, since science is an ongoing process, various paradigms, or parts of paradigms now discredited, may prove to have relevance in the future. Brown points out that "the theory of continental drift, for example, was overwhelmingly rejected by geologists in the 1920's . . . [but] during the past ten years it has been incorporated into the widely accepted theory of plate tectonics."[18]

Once we accept that the sense, or paradigm, of the science of the past retains its validity, we can profitably study it in some of the same ways in which we have profitably studied literature. It might well prove possible, for example, to relate certain features of the phlogiston theory to the thought patterns of the Enlightenment, much as we can relate Dante's cosmology to the thought of Aquinas. Similarly, we can begin to understand both the art and science of a given period as functions of the technology of the time. In English literary history, one can relate Richardson's novels to the printing techniques that created the lending libraries of the late eighteenth century, and those of Dickens to the monthly journals of the nineteenth century. Astronomy and biology use paradigms drawn from the potentialities of instruments for visual observation; the creation of radio telescopes and electron microscopes created revolutions in both disciplines.

Kuhn makes the intriguing comment that "like artists, scientists must occasionally be able to live in a world out of joint."[19] Artists and scientists who respond in innovative ways to what Kuhn calls "the essential tension" in any paradigm are apt to encounter resistance of varying degrees of intensity from their colleagues. Picasso shocked even so fine a painter as Braque with *Les Demoiselles d'Avignon,* and critics called Eliot "a drunken madman" for writing *The Wasteland.* As Kuhn points out, Lord Kelvin denounced Roentgen's discovery of X rays as a hoax,[20] and the German physicists Otto Stern and Max von Laue swore that they would give up physics if Niels Bohr's seminal work on quantum theory in 1913 turned out to have any validity.[21] Reception studies constitute a well-established genre among German critics, and comparative studies of the responses to the scientific and artistic innovations of a given period might well prove a fruitful method for studying cultural history.

The possibility of making such comparisons between the arts and the sciences by utilizing historicism convinces me of the possibility of articulating a general, unified system for relating the arts and the sciences. If such a system is to avoid the inadequacies of Marxism, it must assimilate both the historicism I have suggested above and the epistemology of twentieth-century science. I have neither the space nor the competence to deal adequately with the philosophy of contemporary science, especially with the all-important features of quantum mechanics.[22] Surely we can agree that Albert Einstein and Kurt Goedel rank among the leading theorists of our century, and a paradigm that draws on their work makes a valid beginning.

Einstein stated in *The Principle of Relativity* that

> it is neither the point in space, nor the instant in time, at which something happens that has physical reality, but only the event itself. There is no absolute (independent of the space of reference) relation in time between events.[23]

If "no absolute relation in time between events" exists, there necessarily exists a plurality of time systems, for every event is one with its time system. And a belief in the plurality of time systems means, I believe, the kind of historicism I have been advocating here. Moreover, events—the only reality—have dynamism, not merely movement, and this dynamism comes from an inner coherence that often takes the form of a binary pair, such as the positive and negative poles of an electrical field, matter and antimatter, or the double strands of the DNA molecule. From these relationships, one can derive two pairs of principles: pluralism, which implies incompleteness; and dynamism, which implies a coherence of interrelated entities. The terminological problems endemic to theoretical discussions such as these arise here, of course; perhaps it may suffice for now to emphasize that I do not use the term *pluralism* in the sense in which a social scientist would use it but simply to denote the absence of a privileged, or "objective," frame of reference.

As I understand the term, pluralism implies a contrast between heterogeneous entities, and the contrast itself creates meaning. Though these principles are hardly unique to the twentieth century, our age has used them with unprecedented frequency. By realizing that this is the case, one can find structural similarities among various seminal theorists. For example, the most famous sentence in the book that created the paradigm for structural linguistics, Ferdinand de Saussure's *Course in General Linguistics* (1916), is: *"In the 'langue' there are only differences."*[24] Saussure had in mind such oppositions as the difference between the two words of a minimal pair in phonology, but the Russian Formalist Yury Tynianov made just such a contrast the criterion for the very existence of art:

> But if the feeling of *interaction* of two factors (which pre-supposes the obligatory presence of two moments: a subordinating one and a subordinated one) disappears, the fact of art is erased: it is automatized.[25]

The insistence that a work of art creates a whole by incorporating heterogeneous elements within itself appears elsewhere as well. Sergei Eisenstein's essays on the theory of montage in film express a similar attitude, as does Ezra Pound's definition of a poetic image as "an intellectual or emotional complex." In drama, Bertolt Brecht's idea of *Verfremdungseffekt* calls for a deliberate contrast within the work.

As for dynamism and incompleteness, the most trenchant epistemological arguments in their favor come from Kurt Goedel's paper of 1931, "On Formally Undecidable Propositions of the *Principia Mathematica* and Related Systems." Goedel's Proof, as mathematicians call this paper, along with related work Alonzo Church published in 1936 and some papers by Thoralf Skolem in the 1920s, belongs to metatheory—theory about the nature of theory. All these works of metatheory present proofs of the arbitrariness of the axiomatic method by which Euclidean geometry proceeds. Axioms, we recall, are valid and complete in themselves; by definition, they are not open to question, for they create the paradigm for all subsequent operations. So defined, axioms correspond to other concepts which have come under serious attack (not to say refutation) in the twentieth century, such as uniform time and space in Newtonian physics and the categorical imperative in Kantian philosophy.

Those of us who have not done advanced work in mathematics will never be able even to state Goedel's Proof rigorously, much less follow its reasoning; nevertheless, ordinary language suffices to state the principles involved, and it is the principles that concern us here. Mathematicians call these theorems "limitative theorems," because they state inherent limits on knowledge. In *Goedel's Proof,* Ernst Nagel and James Newman state most forcefully just what this incompleteness means for logic:

> He [Goedel] proved that it is impossible to establish the internal logical consistency of a very large class of deductive systems—elementary arithmetic, for example—unless one adopts principles of reasoning so complex that their internal consistency is as open to doubt as that of the systems themselves.[26]

If complete, i.e., axiomatized, systems are inconsistent, then consistent systems are incomplete. As Jean Piaget has said, "Goedel showed that the construction of a demonstrably consistent relatively rich theory requires not simply an 'analysis' of its 'presuppositions' but the construction of the next higher theory!"[27] Goedel's Proof thus resembles Saussure's linguistics and Tynianov's aesthetics in that it assumes that an interaction between two entities creates meaning and validity. Such an interaction creates a process, and thus Goedel's Proof denies the validity of visual, static images such as the "foundation" or "basis" of knowledge; knowledge exists as a dynamic and thus incomplete system of increasing complexity.

I believe that we can find the elements of a paradigm which will incorporate the desired features of dynamism and incompleteness in Henri Bergson's *Essai sur les données immédiates de la conscience* (1889). In the *Essai* (known in English as *Time and Free Will*), Bergson ponders the implications of the homology between the uniformity of space and the uniformity of time in Newtonian physics. Since time and space exist objectively in this paradigm, their units of measure do not change and are related only by succession. That is to say, each one comes after the previous one and none interacts with any other. Therefore, what Bergson calls "the deeply rooted habit of spreading out time in space" (p. 81),[28] or "spatialization," has become a common habit of visualization that in our day has allowed a translation of time into space such as "historical perspective" to become a cliché. Bergson rejects spatialization because he says that it denies our sense of self-identity. If each moment is truly homogeneous and discrete, he asks, how can we know our past?

Bergson begins the positive aspect of his argument by associating poetry with hypnosis and our reaction to music: "The successive intensities of aesthetic feeling thus correspond to the changes of state which have supervened in us" (p. 16). By "successive," he wishes to emphasize the changes we experience while retaining a single identity. Bergson thus insists on a unity of sensibility that derives from a dynamic multiplicity in a way which anticipates the structure of much modernist art.

In a chapter significantly entitled "Multiplicity of States of Consciousness," Bergson begins an intellectual revolution by using not the *visual* imagery so common in the nineteenth century but *aural* imagery. He says that our experiences are "dissolved together, so to speak, (like) the notes of a melody," and asks: "Could not one say if the notes succeed each other, we nevertheless perceive them in each other, and their totality is comparable to a living being, whose parts, however distinct, interpenetrate through the same effect of the solidarity?" (p. 68). Later he speaks of states that "interpenetrate and organize themselves like the notes of a melody, to form what we call an indistinct or qualitative multiplicity" (p. 70).

The choice of aural imagery necessitates of itself a holistic paradigm; one cannot divide a melody into its parts without destroying it. Moreover, music—and sound in general—is inherently dynamic; it is continually an event in the process of becoming. And, in a manner consistent with the work of Saussure, Tynianov, and others, a melody consists of an "indistinct or qualitative multiplicity." It is a poor melody that has only one note; melody, like meaning itself, derives from the interaction of heterogeneous entities. As David Sipfle has put it, "Bergson denies that time is measurable *because* he denies that it is homogeneous. It is a radical heterogeneity which distinguishes the temporal from the spatial, and there can hardly be heterogeneity without multiplicity *of some sort.*"[29]

Bergson denies the Newtonian dichotomy between rigid space and the hard bodies it contains, for the notes of the melody interpenetrate—the first note has not died out before the second one sounds. An analogy with sound clearly helps more in understanding subatomic physics, with its exotic particles like quarks and even quons, than an attempt to visualize billiard balls bouncing off each other. Hence, so prestigious a scientist as Louis de Broglie, in an intriguing essay, could find that Bergson anticipated certain essential features of contemporary physical theories.[30] Since sight was to Newtonian physics what sound is to Einsteinian physics, an epistemological historicism of the kind I espouse here does not use visual images for conceptual or cognitive purposes.

However, this does not mean that one must take music as paradigmatic of cognition, as Bergson did for memory. The referential quality of language makes the verbal arts more comparable with the arts than with music, as long as we think of language as *spoken* language. Walter Ong makes the important distinction that "sight may provide a great deal of the material to think *about,* but the terms *in* which all men do their thinking corresponds to words, that is to sounds."[31] Ong construes words here as occurring in spoken dialogue, a situation I take as paradigmatic because it involves just the interaction between two entities that an epistemological historicism requires.

If we consider the structure of a spoken utterance, we realize that we can analyze it in at least four different ways; in terms of its phonology, its morphology, its syntax, and its grammar. I wish to offer here a paradigm which utilizes these distinctions, and which may prove fruitful for the study of cultural history. The paradigm, with its analogies to linguistics, takes the following form:

Grammar   Conceptual Paradigms
Syntax: "The Existing Monuments"/Contemporary Science: The Social
                                          Process (individual as part of National)
Morphology: The Corpus of the Artist's/Scientist's Entire Work
Phonology: The Individual Work/The Individual Experiment (or Theorem)

Explication begins at the bottom, with the simplest element, and becomes more complex when it corporates the next higher element, as Goedel's Proof demands.[32]

Although I include all four levels for the sake of completeness, the paradigm works best at the level of syntax, and I will concentrate on this level. Despite Harold Cassidy's explication of the similarities and differences between an equation by Newton and a poem by Francis Thompson,[33] the overall value of such comparison remains uncertain. However, we can emphasize the importance of the phonology level by noticing that problems both in literature and in science which occur at this specific level can sometimes be resolved by moving to the next level, that of morphology.

Brown cites an example involving the reception of Newton's *Principia* that lends itself to just such an interpretation. He notes that "even after Newton did publish *Principia* there were major discrepancies between his theory and the results of observation and experiment. For example, he was aware that the computed value of the motion of the moon's orbit was only half the observed value."[34] However, this one instance of failure did not deter scientists from using Newtonian mechanics, because the totality of the system had demonstrable validity.

E. D. Hirsch's *Validity in Interpretation* offers an analogous example in literary criticism. He notes the discrepancy between two interpretations of Wordsworth's "A Slumber Did My Spirit Seal." Commenting that both the interpretations in question "remain equally coherent and self-sustaining,"[35] he suggests the following factors as decisive between one that emphasizes inconsolability and one more positive:

> Instead of regarding rocks and stones and trees merely as inert objects, he probably regarded them in 1799 as deeply alive, as part of the immortal life of nature. Physical death he felt to be a return to the source of life, a new kind of participation in nature's "revolving immortality." From everything we know of Wordsworth's typical attitudes during the period in which he composed the poem, inconsolability and bitter irony do not belong in its horizon.[36]

It is readily apparent that despite the differences in material,

Hirsch is advocating the same kind of movement from phonology to morphology as that which eighteenth-century scientists more or less unconsciously adopted.

Just as the movement from phonology to morphology involves a generalization, so does the movement from morphology to syntax. The generality at this level requires the inclusion of both professional achievement and personal biography if the paradigm is to avoid a most egregious failing common in Marxist criticism, that of justifying brutality and injustice when committed in the name of the Party. Thus, Stalinism was a "necessary stage" in the development of socialism. Epistemologically, the argument involves two dichotomies—one between the present and the future, and one between individuals and social processes. The paradigm presented here, however, suggests that social processes can occur only through individuals. When individuals become *welthistorisch*—I know of no single English modifier that would include Stalin, Einstein, and Joyce—it means that some homology exists between the individual process and the social process. Erik Erikson's *Young Man Luther* showed how one could fruitfully and nonreductively analyze this mutual homology, and the burgeoning subdiscipline of psychohistory promises similarly to increase our understanding of the dynamics of this crucial relationship. I will offer here two brief examples of such analysis, one from literature and one from science. Each analysis involves the reference of problems of interpretation of a given phenomenon from the individual to the social process. Since we are accustomed to studying literature in terms of social factors, but not science, I will discuss the scientific material at greater length.

The literary example concerns the work of Anton Chekhov and the interpretation of his short stories and plays as "the voice of twilight Russia." The inability of Chekhov's characters, especially his men, to take decisive action or to do anything except sit around and philosophize dreamily about how life will be in a hundred years has been taken as indicative of Chekhov's melancholy personality, which in turn is typical of the mood of the last years of the czarist empire. I take this as an example of an interpretation that suffers from the use of preexisting categories and shows us how *not* to understand the individual process in terms of the national process.

One possible way to bring together Chekhov's life and work would be to note that he was born in 1860, at about the time of the beginning of a great railroad boom in Russia; while the effects of the *appearance* of the railroad resound through the work of Tolstoy and Dostoevsky, Chekhov represented the generation that had grown up with the railroad. But, paradoxically, the effect of the railroads in much of Russia was to make the people in the provinces feel not closer to the big cities but more isolated from them. A trip to the city that had taken a week or so in the past might now take only a day; but this knowledge merely heightened the sense of contrast and isolation rural people—the vast majority of the Russian population at the time—felt. (The government inadvertently heightened this effect by building the stations not in the centers of towns but at some distance from them.) Since the planning of Russian railroad systems did not take into account people's needs and wishes, it seems that this extremely important innovation had the effect of increasing a sense of helplessness and isolation. In thus isolating his characters and having them express their hopelessness and resignation, Chekhov was verbalizing a social process in Russia at the time—whether he knew it or not.

Of course, he was doing more than this as well. He has proved very influential in the English-speaking world, as the short stories of Katherine Mansfield and John Cheever and the plays of Harold Pinter attest. (Woody Allen's recent film *Interiors* was a remake of *The Three Sisters,* done in the style of Bergman's *Cries and Whispers.*) We as Americans will not find such interest in a writer unless he deals with something in our own lives. That is to say, the immediate reference of Chekhov's works, turn-of-the-century Russia, cannot arouse deep emotions; the sense, however, does affect us because the sense involves people who are unhoused and displaced or are in the process of becoming so. Now this is the quintessential American situation, and Chekhov's treatment of it speaks to our own experience.

The scientific example of interpretation at the level of syntax draws on Kuhn's concept of the "essential tension" that necessarily exists, he says, in any scientific theory—a tension between the successes and failures of the theory. Any theory that can generate research does so because it creates ways of dealing with certain phenomena, which become research problems. But practicing scientists can never completely predict which research problems will prove intractable and become counterinstances that nothing but a revolution can explain. I submit that the social process (or some part of it, in large countries) can condition the emphases of scientists who engage in basic research. Indeed, some work on the sociology of science has already produced suggestive results in this regard. For example, Harriet Zuckerman, in her study of American Nobel laureates in science, has shown that Jewish scientists are far more likely to have received the prize for theoretical work than Protestant laureates, whose prize-winning research generally dealt with practical problems.[37] The work of both groups of scientists thus expressed the emphases of their respective cultural milieux. It needs emphasis, though, that such patterns have meaning only for fairly large samples and not for individual cases.

As an example of a statistical, noncausal, indeterminate relationship between the social process and scientific theory, let us consider the differing interpretations of quantum mechanics in Germany and Russia. Quantum mechanics, the study of the behavior of electrons in their orbits around a nucleus, has been called the most important scientific revolution of all time and has attracted some of the finest minds of this or any other century. I will make no attempt to discuss this extremely technical and abstruse topic, except to say that the issue of causality, an essential feature of Newtonian mechanics, rapidly became a crucial one and the occasion for widespread disagreement and debate.

In a remarkable study, Paul Forman has investigated the relationship between the intellectual climate of Weimar Germany and the theories of its physicists. He begins by contrasting the optimism of the German scientific community in the summer of 1918 with its pessimism and despair in the fall, when defeat came so suddenly to Germany. The German scientists believed, rightly, that the prestige of their discipline had remained high because of their contribution to a seemingly successful war effort and that it would fall when that war effort failed. As literature uses the socially conditioned medium of language, so twentieth-century physics uses the socially conditioned language of money; research possibilities thus depend in part on the social standing of the discipline.

But in postwar Germany the standing of physicists fell very low, and Oswald Spengler's *The Decline of the West* codified the antiintellectual, antiscientific mood of those years. Significantly, Spengler used an opposition between causality and destiny: "Over and over again Spengler equates causality, conceptual analysis, and physics, and flays them across the stage of world history."[38] And, since the general public identified causality and physics, the scientists considered a reconstruction in their

discipline highly necessary. Forman puts the relationship between the social context and the actual theoretical work which
led to the formulation of what historians now call "the second
quantum theory" very well:

> The nature of that reconstruction was itself virtually dictated by the
> general intellectual environment: if the physicist were to improve
> his public image he had first and foremost to dispense with causal-
> ity, with rigorous determinism, that most universally abhorred fea-
> ture of the physical world picture. And this, of course, turned out
> to be precisely what was required for the solution of those problems
> in atomic physics which were then at the focus of the physicists'
> interest.[39]

This is not to say, however, that Werner Heisenberg's matrix
mechanics in the fall of 1925 and Erwin Schrödinger's wave
mechanics in the spring of 1926 excluded causality from the
physical universe once and for all. Einstein himself, for example, resisted this conclusion until his death, and numerous
other major scientists have attempted to reconcile quantum mechanics with causality. Nowhere, however, have scientists done
so with greater consistency than in Russia; and in Russia, as in
Germany, scientists pursued their work in a manner consistent
with—yet not necessarily subject to—public opinion.

One must make certain distinctions in comparing the situation of scientists in postwar Germany with that of scientists in
postrevolutionary Russia. By 1930, no public opinion existed in
Russia—only governmental opinion. And one needs to distinguish carefully between the crude rhetoric of the official newspapers and the work of people who truly believed in dialectical
materialism. For such people, the postrevolutionary period
meant a surge of optimism that one could build a socialist state.
Moreover, if we keep in mind that the Soviet Union gives major
scientists the kinds of perquisites and prestige that American
society accords rock stars, one can readily understand why a
sincere Marxist scientist would argue for the retention of causality in quantum mechanics. Lenin, in *Materialism and Empirio-
Criticism,* fiercely denounced any abandonment of classical
physics; the society that had so generously rewarded the scientist needed the principle of causality in order to modernize a
dreadfully backward country.

Thus, when Loren Graham analyzes the attitudes toward
causality among major Soviet physicists in his important *Science
and Philosophy in the Soviet Union,* he finds these scientists unan-

imous in their adherence to causality. Graham's demonstration of consistency in this matter carries all the more weight because he cites works written both before and after Stalin's death. One major Soviet physicist, Dmitry Blokhintsev, dealt with the problem by distinguishing between Laplacian determinism and causality: "Within the context of this understanding of causality Blokhintsev considered quantum mechanics causal."[40] Another physicist of comparable stature, Vladimir Fock, retained causality in quantum mechanics by making some distinctions:

> Realizing that a microdescription of microparticles would be different from the classical description of the same particles, we can say that on both levels (micro and macro-) the principle of causality holds. Since we always use a macro-description, however, we should redefine causality in such a way that it fits both levels. . . . The true absence of causality in nature would mean to Fock that not even probabilistic descriptions could be given; all outcomes would be equally probable.[41]

In short, Russian scientists have consistently equated causality with science itself.

One should keep in mind here that quantum mechanics is a discipline without definite answers and principles; scientists all over the world disagree about it and many scientists both inside and outside of Russia also believe that quantum mechanics retains causality. Yet, it does seem clear that some subtle, indirect social factors gave the scientists of Weimar Germany and Soviet Russia a certain predisposition to adopt differing attitudes on the issue of causality.

As the name of one of the pairs of elements on the left side of the syntactic level, "The Existing Monuments," suggests, this level incorporates and systematizes T. S. Eliot's essay "Tradition and the Individual Talent." One can interpret this famous statement as an exercise that applies the principles of incompleteness and dynamism in a way relevant to both literature and to science.

A well-known sentence from "Tradition and the Individual Talent" reads: "No poet, no artist of any sort, has his complete meaning alone" (p. 14.)[42] That is, he or she remains incomplete without the tradition. The obvious tradition, the tradition of the artist's country, also remains incomplete unless one understands it as part of "the whole of the literature of Europe from Homer" (p. 4). Pound would have said, "the literature of Europe and Asia." In insisting on a knowledge of world litera-

ture for the poet, Eliot was in effect making him something like
a scientist. Science has always been more international than
literature, because it deals primarily in abstractions and easily
translatable principles; in a multilingual age—and, moreover,
in an age when various writers such as Nabokov, Borges, and
Beckett have written in more than one language—
cosmopolitanism becomes a pressing need for the writer as
well.

Eliot's "ideal order" exists as process:

> In order to persist after the supervention of novelty, the *whole*
> existing order must be, if ever so slightly, altered; and so the rela-
> tions, proportions, values of each work of art toward the whole are
> readjusted. [P. 5]

Significantly, a substitution of the phrase "current paradigm"
for "the whole existing order" makes very little difference in
this statement. As Kuhn emphasizes, paradigms are constantly
evolving, and they will tolerate scientific novelties, or
anomalies, only so long. The truly significant novelty requires
an adjustment of the paradigm as a whole.

Therefore, Eliot concludes, "the historical sense involves a
perception, not only of the pastness of the past, but of its presence" (p. 4). This definition of the historical sense strikingly
resembles Bergson's analysis of perception as interpolating the
past into the present. While the science of a hundred years ago
does not affect a scientist as directly as the literature of a hundred years ago affects a writer, the scientist of today clearly
needs an awareness of the nature and function of the scientific
revolutions of the past, for without it he may become rigid and
believe that the current form of the paradigm expresses some
final truth about nature, while in fact it gives only one version
of that truth.

Greater difficulties for literature arise from Eliot's assertions
"Poetry is not a turning loose of emotion, but an escape from
emotion; it is not the expression of personality, but an escape
from personality" (p. 18) and "the emotion of art is impersonal"
(p. 9). People have generally thought of science as impersonal
truth, but not poetry. The principal problem here derives from
Eliot's use of "impersonal," which implies an opposition to
"personal." However, if we rewrite "impersonal" as "suprapersonal," we can relate the creation of literature to the creation of
meaning through language. If we rewrite "poet" (or scientist) as

"speaker," and "poetry" (or science) as "language," then "Tradition and the Individual Talent" seems remarkably similar to Saussure's *Course,* which had come out the previous year (1916).

The fourth element, "Conceptual Paradigms," consists of the first three elements taken as a totality, for interpretation, and cognition in general, can come only from paradigms that people have internalized during their individual developmental processes, and these in turn express and affect the social process from which the paradigms come. "But," as David Bloor puts it, "the theoretical component of knowledge is precisely the social component."[43] Thus, articulation must cease here, for people cannot fully articulate or describe any totality in which they themselves participate. Ultimately, one cannot analyze one's own paradigms, except in the process of undergoing a gestalt switch, which will make them part of one's past. And since critics, scientists, and writers all use conceptual paradigms that belong to the social processes of their time, the system is reflexive on itself; it is not closed, however, because each individual experiences only part of the totality. The system therefore remains incomplete, dynamic, and open.

This incompleteness of the level of grammar maintains Kuhn's "essential tension" in paradigms, and thereby expresses the inherent limitations on knowledge that Goedel's Proof postulates. Throughout this paper, I have emphasized the importance of paradigms, because I believe that only in terms of paradigms can one hope to interrelate the arts and the sciences, as well as other disparate activities. If all meaningful behavior requires a paradigm, as I believe it does, then both art and science use paradigms, and the use of epistemological historicism involves articulating those paradigms.

One can understand art and science as related activities by attributing more objectivity to art than critics usually do, and by attributing to science more arbitrariness than philosophers of science usually do. Art acquires the only valid objectivity, that of consensus, by having what Anthony Savile calls an "essentially public nature." Savile states of artistic masterpieces that "it is a precondition of our being able to talk of them as expressions of mastery that we think of them as governed by, and accessible to, publicly known or publicly discoverable rules of propriety."[44] And it is just such "publicly known or publicly discoverable rules of propriety" that constitute the paradigms of scientific research. That a much smaller group of people have internalized scientific paradigms than artistic ones does not invalidate the essential similarity.

Savile makes another point about the arts which applies to science. He says that we may not be able to choose between interpretations of a work, in which case "the work is simply indeterminate in its canonical interpretation, and we should not be surprised to find that this may be so."[45] As art may be indeterminate, so may science; quantum mechanics offers an extremely important case in point.

If the use of paradigms in the arts and in the sciences means that they have both a certain objectivity and a certain arbitrariness, then they have some of the qualities of spoken language, and the analysis of language may serve as a metaphorical paradigm for understanding them in related ways. The use of language in spoken dialogue has just the qualities of dynamism, incompleteness, and arbitrariness that epistemological historicism—a historicism which denies the validity of the visual paradigm of Newtonian physics—requires. A true historicism, moreover, requires an awareness of the way in which Goedel's Proof postulates increasing complexity; as Jacques Derrida puts it:

> If we wanted to conceive and classify all the metaphorical possibilities of philosophy, there would always be at least one metaphor which would be excluded and remain outside the system; that one, at least, which was needed to construe the concept of metaphor, or, to cut the argument short, the metaphor of metaphor of metaphor.[46]

1. Jeffrey Sammons, *Literary Sociology and Practical Criticism* (Bloomington, Ind.: Indiana University Press, 1977), p. 17.

2. Ibid., p. 21.

3. V. I. Lenin, *Polnoe sobranie sochinenii*, 5th ed., 55 vols. (Moscow: State Publishing House for Political Literature, 1958–65), 18:192. Unless otherwise cited, translations are my own.

4. Ibid., p. 195.

5. For some striking analogies to Lenin's political use of Newton, see Margaret C. Jacob, *The Newtonians and the English Revolution, 1689–1720* (Ithaca, N.Y.: Cornell University Press, 1976.)

6. Milič Čapek, *The Philosophical Impact of Contemporary Physics* (Princeton, N.J.: Van Nostrand, 1961), p. 124.

7. See David Caute's remarks on Lucien Goldmann in *The Illusion* (New York: Harper & Row, 1972), pp. 155ff.

8. Sammons, *Literary Sociology*, pp. 23–24.

9. Ibid., p. 161.

10. Thomas S. Kuhn, *The Structure of Scientific Revolutions,* 2d ed., rev. (Chicago: University of Chicago Press, 1970), p. 1.

11. Ibid., p. 158.

12. Harold Brown, *Perception, Theory, and Commitment* (Chicago: Precedent, 1977), p. 151.

13. Ibid., p. 165.

14. Čapek, *Philosophical Impact of Contemporary Physics,* p. 4.

15. Stendhal [pseud.], *Romans et nouvelles* (Paris: Gallimard, 1947), p. 286.

16. Page numbers after quotations from Frege's "On Sense and Reference" refer to *Translations from the Philosophical Writings of Gottlob Frege,* ed. Peter Geach and Max Black (Oxford: Basil Blackwell, 1960).

17. Kuhn, *Structure of Scientific Revolutions,* p. 100.

18. Brown, *Perception, Theory, and Commitment,* p. 153.

19. Kuhn, *Structure,* p. 79.

20. Ibid., p. 59.

21. See Friedrich Hund, *The History of Quantum Theory* (New York: Barnes and Noble, 1974), p. 74.

22. Max Jammer says: "Never before in the history of science has there been a theory which has had such a profound impact on human thinking as quantum mechanics." Max Jammer, *The Philosophy of Quantum Mechanics* (New York: Wiley, 1974), p. v.

23. Albert Einstein, *The Meaning of Relativity,* 5th ed. (Princeton, N.J.: Princeton University Press, 1955), pp. 30–31.

24. Ferdinand de Saussure, *Cours de linguistique générale* (Paris: Payot, 1960), p. 166.

25. Yury Tynianov, *Problema stikhotvornogo yazyka* (1924; reprint ed., The Hague: Mouton, 1963), p. 10.

26. Ernst Nagel and James Newman, *Goedel's Proof* (New York: New York University Press, 1970), p. 34.

27. Jean Piaget, *Structuralism,* ed. and trans. Chaninah Maschler (New York: Basic Books, 1970), p. 34.

28. Page numbers after quotations from Bergson refer to: Henri Bergson, *Oeuvres* (Paris: PUF, 1959).

29. David A. Sipfle, "Henri Bergson and the Epochal Theory of Time," in *Bergson and the Evolution of Physics,* ed. Peter Gunter (Knoxville, Tenn.: University of Tennessee Press, 1969), p. 280.

30. Louis de Broglie, "The Concepts of Contemporary Physics and Bergson's Ideas on Time and Motion," *Bergson and the Evolution of Physics,* pp. 45–61.

31. Walter J. Ong, S.J., *The Presence of the Word* (New Haven, Conn.: Yale University Press, 1967), p. 140.

32. Note, however, one major distinction: Roman Jakobson has commented that in language freedom of choice increases as one moves from phonology (where there is virtually no choice) to morphology, to syntax, to grammar (where there is considerable choice). See Roman Jakobson, "Two Aspects of Language: Metaphor and Metonymy," in *European Literary Theory and Practice,* ed. Vernon W. Gras (New York: Delta, 1973), pp. 120–21.

33. See Harold Cassidy, *The Sciences and the Arts: A New Alliance* (New York: Harper, 1962).

34. Brown, *Perception, Theory, and Commitment,* p. 96.

35. E. D. Hirsch, *Validity in Interpretation* (New Haven: Yale University Press, 1967), p. 239.

36. Ibid.

37. Harriet Zuckerman, *Scientific Elite: Nobel Laureates in the United States* (New York: Free Press, 1977), p. 77.

38. Paul Forman, "Weimar Culture, Causality, and Quantum Theory, 1918–1927: Adaptation by German Physicists and Mathematicians to a Hostile Intellectual Environment," *Historical Studies in the Physical Sciences* 3 (1971): 33.

39. Ibid., pp. 7–8.

40. Loren R. Graham, *Science and Philosophy in the Soviet Union* (New York: Knopf, 1972), p. 90.

41. Ibid., p. 98.

42. Page numbers after quotations from "Tradition and the Individual Talent" refer to T. S. Eliot, *Selected Essays. 1917–1932* (New York: Harcourt Brace, 1932).

43. David Bloor, *Knowledge and Social Imagery* (London: Routledge and Kegan Paul, 1976), p. 86.

44. Anthony Savile, "Historicity and the Hermeneutic Circle," *New Literary History* 10, no. 1 (Autumn 1978): 55.

45. Ibid., p. 63.

46. Jacques Derrida, "White Mythology: Metaphor in the Text of Philosophy," *New Literary History* 6, no. 1 (Autumn 1974): 18.

Practical
Approaches

Res et Verba: Scriblerian Satire and the Fate of Language

Roger D. Lund

LeMoyne College

SCHOLARS have generally agreed that Thomas Sprat's *History of the Royal Society* (1667) served as a virtual manifesto for that minor linguistic revolution since come to be known as the reformation of seventeenth-century prose style.[1] Of course Sprat was not the first to have called for a leaner style more suited to the demands of a new scientific methodology of empirical observation and accurate reporting, but it was Sprat whose enthusiasm and rhetorical skill gave life and force to the idea that the language of scientific description should be clearly differentiated from literary language, insisting that the writers of natural philosophy "turn back to the primitive purity, and shortness, when men delivered so many *things* almost in an equal number of words . . . bringing all as near the Mathematical plainness as they can."[2] While Sprat's program was obviously more influential on the writers of scientific works,[3] it had indirect effects on imaginative literature as well, particularly the satires written by the members of the Scriblerus circle—Pope, Swift, Arbuthnot, Gay, and Parnell—who responded with peculiar zest and consistency to the notion that words and things are interchangeable and to Sprat's equally vexing proposition that the mathematical method should be adopted as a model for prose.[4] In short, I would suggest that this Scriblerian fascination with the metaphorical equation of words and things is a centrally important feature of their ironic defense of the right uses of the English language and of English literature, and is the motive force behind one of their most characteristic rhetorical strategies: the literalization of metaphor. Perhaps most curious, however, is the degree to which the satires of the Scriblerians seem to predict recent developments in theories of language and literature, to reflect, as it were, a kind of fun-house image of the shape of language theory in our own time.

I do not mean to suggest that there is any direct correlation between the Scriblerians and modern language theory or to imply that the Scriblerians themselves were theorists in any sense. Hostile to all forms of arbitrary systematizing in others, Pope and Swift are defiantly unsystematic in their own non-satirical discussions of language, when they discuss it at all. Pope's dictum that "expression is the dress of thought" is perfectly conventional wisdom, and Swift's "theory of language" expressed in the *Proposal for Correcting the English Tongue* is largely a plea for some means of fixing a language in transition, of preserving its intelligibility in an age of change.[5] There is, however, more method in their treatment of language in the inverted world of satire where we encounter the consistent reductio ad absurdum of the notion that words are but things. This pattern is a response to the growing popularity of various forms of mechanistic philosophy, promulgated by Hobbes, Descartes, Lucretius, and even Locke, which suggested (however faintly) that man was but a machine, and that speech and reason were themselves the products of purely mechanical processes. Sprat's attempt to conflate words and things was viewed by the Scriblerians as a linguistic embodiment of this larger mechanistic threat. It is this pattern that I wish to examine here.[6] If we step outside the immediate historical context of Scriblerian satire, however, we discover that at the level of historical analogy and ironic prophecy the Scriblerian treatment of the word as thing also reveals that what for them was the stuff of nightmares has become for us the raw material of popular forms of modern criticism. One might argue that part of the pleasure in reading such texts as *Gulliver's Travels* or the *Memoirs of Martinus Scriblerus* resides in this shock of recognition.

If we hear the echoes of modern debates over structuralism, cybernetics, or semiotics in the mad arguments of Scriblerian heroes, they are, of course, only echoes from another age; yet there are significant points of comparison. Certainly the

Scriblerians recognized the interdependence of man and his language, understanding that it is speech that makes reason possible and sets man apart from the rest of creation. And while they had almost certainly absorbed the notion implicit in the Classical *episteme* that words are but signs which represent things,[7] there are lingering traces of that venerable tradition which located the origins of the gift of language in man's special creation by God himself, and in Adam's original role as the assigner of names. It seems equally likely that Pope and Swift also accepted the idea (here succinctly outlined by George Steiner) that "the exercise of human language enacts, albeit on a microscopically humble scale, the Divine reflex of creation, the *Logos* or 'speaking into being' of the universe."[8] In a more practical sense, they recognized that man's identity is related to his use of language and they understood in some shadowy fashion that "language forms quite literally underlie and perpetuate human behavior."[9] The argument consistently embodied in Scriblerian satire is that a mechanical language produces mechanical men, and vice versa. So it is, one might argue, that the Scriblerians react so violently against the notion that the spiritual springs of language might be replaced by lifeless mechanism, that the word made flesh might indeed become the word made thing. So it is that they decry the corruption of literary language in the hands of dull poets, accusing them of rendering it metaphorically, if not actually lifeless. And so it is, finally, that the Scriblerians fall so heavily on Sprat's rather simple proposals for stylistic reform, proposals which in their more general outlines seemed to mine the very foundations upon which man's special status as a language animal had always rested.

As one would expect from such an inveterate ironist, Swift's response to Sprat is consistently parodic and ironically indirect, dramatically embodying in mock-panegyric those very ideas he most distrusted. In Book 3 of *Gulliver's Travels*, containing a series of episodes that mock the whole scientific enterprise of the Royal Society, Swift clearly parodies Sprat's linguistic program in the description of a new project to "shorten Discourse by cutting Polysyllables into one, and leaving out Verbs and Participles; because in Reality all things imaginable are but Nouns."[10] Since Swift's treatment of all theories, scientific and nonscientific, tended to isolate and project their moral and practical consequences, it seems fitting that we should be given a demonstration of this program in action. "Since words are only Names for *Things*," the projectors conclude, "it would be more convenient for all Men to carry about them, such *Things* as were necessary to express the particular Business they are to discourse on" (p. 185). The results are predictably ludicrous and impractical. Says Gulliver, "I have often beheld two of those Sages almost sinking under the Weight of their Packs, like Pedlars among us; who when they met in the streets would lay down their Loads, open their sacks, and hold conversation" (p. 185). Swift had inherited an "ontological view" of language in which individual words stood for things in the real world,[11] but here that metaphorical relationship is radically dislocated for the purposes of satire as Swift literalizes significant metaphor, substituting the literal thing for the word that previously had identified it.[12] Words do not give names to things anymore; they *are* the things themselves. This pattern of literalized metaphor is of central importance in Scriblerian satire, for by it Pope and Swift embody their anxieties that in the rapidly changing intellectual and literary climate of the eighteenth century, words were becoming more like things as men become more like machines, incapable of abstract reasoning or sustained discourse.

It is perhaps ironic, then, that the literal "plainness of speech" practiced by the projectors of Lagado should seemingly have been adopted by those modern writers of concrete poetry. Working to make of the poem a visual object that must be experienced by the senses as words, lines, spaces, and typography, all of which are meant to be absorbed in their totality, the concrete poet seeks to manipulate the "literal object" on the page,[13] rather than trying to use words as signs of some other spiritual or abstract principle. Like those great bags of things carried by the unfortunate projectors of Lagado, concrete poetry approximates as nearly as it can the condition of thingness. Many concrete poems simply dispense with words altogether, depending instead for their significance on such abstract signs as arrows.[14] In the words of a recent apologist for this kind of poetry, "in concrete poetry the word and the thing signified are one,"[15] a view of poetry that would have made Swift shudder. It is not surprising, therefore, that this theory of poetry should also arise out of that mechanized view of the world which Swift found so threatening. "The world as such poetic metaphors present it," writes Abbie W. Beiman, "is a finite entity composed of sensorily perceivable objects, tangible things and knowable facts."[16]

We encounter a similarly contemporary pattern in Swift's objections to Sprat's assertion that prose should be brought as "near the Mathematical plainness" as possible. In the antics of the Laputans, whose "Ideas are perpetually conversant in Lines and Figures" (p. 163), who carefully carve their roasts into geometrical shapes but who cannot cut a decent suit of clothes, Swift dramatizes in a rather homely fashion the practical results of confusing words with numerical signs. As a practical moralist, Swift warns of dire consequences that will arise from attempts to model speech on the structures of mathematics, ironically dramatizing the intellectual and aesthetic lunacy that grows out of the Laputans' mathematical obsession: "If they would, for Example, praise the Beauty of a Woman, or any other Animal, they describe it by Rhombs, Circles, Parallelograms, Ellipses, and other Geometrical Terms" (p. 163). And while their minds are wholly immersed in the terminology of mathematics and the pseudomathematical jargon of Pythagorean music, "Imagination, Fancy and Invention they are wholly Strangers to, nor have any Words in their Language by which those Ideas can be expressed; the whole Compass of their Thoughts and Mind, being shut up within the two forementioned Sciences" (p. 163).[17] Swift's ironic dramatization suggests that in the increasing popularity of the mathematical model, a model that had already been applied to language by Hobbes and Wilkins, he perceived a threat to the primacy of language as man's spiritual signature, as a form of the logos.[18] Only a world from which spirit had been banished could be adequately described by lines and numerals. One also detects an implicit charge that Sprat's program promised nothing less than the violent bifurcation of the language of science and the language of literature, thus isolating the outer world of mechanical nature from the inner world of imaginative experience. And one may even find in Swift's response to Sprat's rather innocent and simple remarks the clear beginnings of that split between science and the humanities grown famous in our own time as the "two cultures."[19]

It seems curiously appropriate, then, that modern linguists and critics have chosen the mathematical model for language study as one means by which this split might be repaired. Of course the field of linguistic and critical study has grown to immense proportions in recent years and my space here is limited; still, certain brief observations may profitably be offered. Certainly the most obvious and significant point of comparison between the state of modern language theory and the satires of Swift is the degree to which his prediction concerning the eventual adoption of the mathematical model has been fulfilled. The primary unifying feature of language study and literary theory since Saussure has been the reliance upon the mathematical equation as the conceptual model for language analysis. Whether one looks to Lévi-Strauss's study of myths with its attempt to sort out structural patterns from a body of data arranged like some random series of integers,[20] or to the structural semantics of Greimas with its attempt to account for the meaning of sentences with the same kind of scientific certainty usually reserved for the laws of nature,[21] or to the rather bizarre theories of Etienne Souriau, who sets out to analyze the drama in hieroglyphic equations,[22] we recognize a common agreement as to the need for a method of linguistic description that owes more to mathematics than to literature as Swift would have known it. One might argue, in fact, that the development of semiology as a "science of signs" reflects an understanding of the function of language and literature to which the Scriblerians could only have responded with hostility.[23]

One of the manifestations of their anxiety over the conflation of words and things was the Scriblerians' exploitation of an ironic science of signs all their own, what one might call a physics of language. We encounter this treatment of the word in *A Tale of a Tub*, where Swift's ironic persona (himself presumably a modern mechanist) offers a "true natural Solution" to the question of why stages are placed above the audience in the theater. According to this "Physico-logical Scheme of Oratorial Receptacles or Machines," a title which in itself merges the ideas of words and things:

> Air being a heavy Body, and therefore (according to the System of *Epicurus*) continually descending, must needs be more so, when loaden and press'd down by Words; which are also Bodies of much Weight and Gravity, as it is manifest from those deep Impressions they make and leave upon us; and therefore must be delivered from a due Altitude, or else they will neither carry a good Aim, nor fall with sufficient Force.[24]

Parodying the Epicurean hypothesis that atoms plummet through the void as a result of their weight and the corollary notion that words themselves are composed of atoms, "bodies of much weight," and therefore subject to the laws that govern other sorts of matter, Swift ridicules the more general mechanistic hypothesis that words might be said to have physical properties or purely mechanical origins.[25] This satirical pattern is more fully developed as Swift's persona explains that different classes of listeners are placed at various levels in the theater itself because "the whining Passions, and little starved Conceits, are gently wafted up by their own extreme Levity, to the middle Region and there fix and are frozen by the frigid Understandings of the Inhabitants. Bombast and Buffoonery, by Nature lofty and light, soar highest of all" (p. 61). In modern terms, what we have here is a burlesque version of affective stylistics, as Swift ironically accounts for the responses of the audience based upon the physical properties of specific classes of words. By so doing, he puts us in mind of such classic structuralist accounts of the affects of words, letters, and syllables as those of Jakobson and Lévi-Strauss, whose microscopic analysis of the emotional responses inspired by the proliferation of nasals and liquids in Baudelaire's "Les Chats" accounts, as it were, for the velocity or levity of particular sounds.[26]

In Swift's ironic literalization of such key words as "bodies," "weight," "gravity," "levity," "aim," "force," and "altitude," ambiguous terms that connote either purely physical or more abstract qualities of language, one discovers the basis of the "anti-mechanist joke" that is repeated throughout *Peri Bathous; or The Art of Sinking in Poetry* with its characteristic emphases on patterns of rising and falling,[27] as well as in the *Dunciad*, where Pope stresses the sheer physicality of the language of dull poets: "And ductile dulness new meanders takes."[28] The metaphor of *ductile* dulness (a word drawn straight from the lexicons of the new science) suggests that words, like metals, are literally malleable. And freed from the constraints enforced by the forming power of the poetic imagination, governed only by the mazy motion of Epicurean chance, words in the *Dunciad* all too frequently behave as if they were only things: "How random thoughts now meaning chance to find, / Now leave all memory of sense behind" (1:275–76). Even the utter nonsense of a Cibber may be described as a "precipitate, like running lead" that slips "thro' cracks and zig-zags of the Head" (1:123–24). The idiocy of Grub Street hacks is not the only abuse of language to suffer this kind of attack in the *Dunciad;* other forms of learning fall victim as well. In Book 4 the ghost of Dr. Busby, once pedantic headmaster of Westminster School, reappears to describe yet another mechanical method of transforming words into things: "Since Man from beast by Words is

known, / Words are Man's province, Words we teach alone. . . .
We ply the Memory, we load the brain, Bind rebel Wit, and
double chain on chain" (4:149–58). While Busby pays homage
to the traditional argument that words are man's spiritual signature, the human equivalent of the Divine logos, he actually
treats them as if they were brute matter. As Aubrey Williams
has so aptly observed, this kind of pedantic emphasis on empty
verbal form that arbitrarily divides words from ideas, confining
the thought while loading the brain, is analogous to Sprat's
attempt to substitute words for things, slighting the "theory
that sense *informs* words, like the soul the body."[29] Certainly
there is a curiously modern air to Busby's remarks, almost an
echo of the modern emphasis on the study of words themselves
as self-reflexive systems, cut off from all relationship with the
world itself. In the very metaphors that modern critics use to
describe language, we detect an agreement that as words have
come to be studied in isolation, they have also become more like
things. When, for example, Robert Scholes discusses Jakobson's
treatment of the relationship between the code and the context,
he speaks of the "growing palpability of message, what one
might call thickening into poetry."[30] And in all discussions of
the "materiality" of the text we seem to find traces of the
Scriblerian treatment of words as objects with their own dimensions, weight, gravity, and force.[31] As Foucault and others have
observed, in the age of Pope, language was a "transparency";
one saw through the word to the object it signified, but in the
"nineteenth and twentieth centuries language has taken on a
substance, weight, an opacity," as we study "its laws just as other
scientists study the laws of material beings."[32]

At the same time our investigations of language have led us
to focus on its materiality, the science of cybernetics has ex-
plored those languages used by machines and their relation to
human communication. Norbert Wiener's blunt assertion that
"in a certain sense, all communications systems terminate in
machines, but that ordinary language systems terminate in the
special sort of machine known as a human being,"[33] seems to
confirm the Scriblerians' most terrible suspicions that man
would eventually come to be defined in purely mechanical
terms. In their satires, this anxiety is most clearly embodied in
images of automata, machinelike men who spit out words as if
they were bits of metal: "As forc'd from wind-guns, lead itself
can fly, / And pond'rous slugs cut swiftly through the sky"
(1:181–82). This description of Cibber as word machine is one

endorsed by the poet himself as he describes the mechanical operation of his own poetic genius: "As clocks to weight their nimble notion owe, / The wheels above urg'd by the load below" (1:183–84). Such images of wheels and clockwork serve as powerful symbols for that new mechanical model of human physiology briefly suggested by Hobbes but more fully articulated by Descartes. They are images etched in extraordinary detail in chapter 12 of the *Memoirs of Martinus Scriblerus,* where the "Society of Freethinkers" describes the creation of a "Hydraulic Engine" or "Artificial Man" who, of course, possesses no soul but who can "walk, and speak, and perform most of the outward actions of the animal life."[34] Whether they speak of words as leaden slugs or as trivial manifestations of the outward mechanical life, the Scriblerians reveal a consistent, if anxious, fascination with *"mechanical Explication*[s] *of Perception or Thinking"* (p. 138) and their relationship to the sources of language.

In *Gulliver's Travels* Swift actually describes the logical conclusion of the mechanization of the word: the complete replacement of linguistic man by machine. The word machine of Lagado is described to Gulliver in glowing terms as yet another project for "improving speculative Knowledge by practical and mechanical Operations" (p. 182), a phrase that ironically embodies Swift's contempt for all short cuts to wisdom as it associates the linguistic program of the Royal Society with the aims of the new mechanistic philosophy. The machine itself works as follows: first, all of the words of the language are printed on papers in "their several Moods, Tenses, Declensions, but without any Order." Placed on dies within a frame, these bits of information can be turned at random to produce the occasional phrase and the rare sentence. By combining these fragments, the "most ignorant Person at a reasonable Charge, and with a little bodily Labour, may write Books in Philosophy, Poetry, Politics, Law, Mathematics, and Theology" (p. 182). Here all assertion that words are informed by sense or that they bear any relation to the world beyond themselves is abandoned in Swift's ironic *reductio* of the notion that since words are but things, they can be produced as easily by machines as by men. At the level of common mythology, this image still retains uncommon power. Men fear the computer as a potential rival in the marketplace and as an even more insidious replacement for their own purely human intelligence. At the level of linguistics or cybernetics, there are familiar echoes as well, as Swift creates his own rough model of information management and anticipates the method of modern linguistics, which seeks to break language down into its smallest elements (here words, not phonemes or morphemes) in order to isolate structures of meaning. Of course, the ultimate mechanization of literature would be poetry produced entirely by machines, and as if they had Swift in mind, various modern poets have experimented with the writing of Fortran poetry on computer tape. "The result," according to one of its advocates, is "mechanized metaphor."[35]

This analogy between mind and machine is worked out in slightly different terms in *Peri Bathous,* where Pope describes a number of mechanical devices designed to assist the modern poet in the art of sinking, among them a "spinning Wheel of the *Bathos,* which draws out and spreads it in the finest thread"[36] as well as a poetical "diving Engine" (p. 15), and a bakery oven where Scriblerus's "Receipt to Make an Epic Poem" can be given a practical test. These metaphors drawn from the realm of applied science are related, I think, to the Scriblerians' sense that they were witnessing the transformation of the art of writing from a genteel and essentially amateur pursuit into a new form of literary manufacturing. In Scriblerus's remarks recommending increased poetic efficiency, we find an uncannily modern conflation of metaphors of imagination and industrial mass production as he recommends that in order to produce faster, modern poets should pool their labors, building an assembly line of poesy:

> For instance, in *Clock-making,* one Artist makes the Balance, another the Spring, another the Crown-Wheels, a fourth the Case, and the principal Workman puts it all together; To this OEconomy we owe the Perfection of our modern Watches; and doubtless we also might that of our modern Poetry. [P. 72][37]

The commonplace of Augustan critical wisdom that called for the poet to "assemble his materials" has here been literalized into the mechanical collection and assemblage of those new industrial raw materials known as words. Once poetry comes to be seen as a mere commodity, the question of popular consumption must also be taken into account, and the Scriblerians are tireless in their attacks on Grub Street poets as the purveyors of disposable trash to be consumed by an ignorant if voracious reading public. It is no accident that both Pope and Swift call attention to the sheer quantity of modern literature that drops stillborn from the press, and to the fate that attends all those poems whisked into pie tins and privies. Of course the real mass production of literature had not yet begun during the lifetime of the Scriblerians themselves, so they seem extraordinarily sensitive to an infant system of publishing that might one day allow the *New York Times* to write, edit, and produce a book-length treatment of news events less than three days old. The Scriblerians were spared the confusion of an age of media; yet it is perhaps not too outrageous to assert that even with their limited optics they had obtained at least a fleeting glimpse of the immensity of the Gutenberg Galaxy.[38]

Pope and Swift attack the Grub Street poets as hacks and operatives whose works are little more than mass-produced junk. And just as they are ridiculed as mechanical producers, so they are indicted as literal consumers. In *A Tale of a Tub,* for example, Swift ironically explains that when words fall downwards from the stage, "that whatever *weighty* Matter shall be delivered thence (whether it be *Lead* or *Gold*) may fall plum into the Jaws of certain *Criticks* . . . which stand ready open to devour them" (p. 61). One may observe here that the reduction of words to things, the Scriblerian physics of language, is also elaborated in somatic metaphors making it a physiology of language as well. Words are described both as weighty matter subject to the laws of gravity and as substances to be consumed and absorbed by the body. In the *Tale,* Swift also describes that elixir which when snuffed up the nose produces in the brain "an infinite Number of Abstracts, Summaries, Compendiums . . . *and the like, all disposed into great Order, and reducible upon Paper*" (p. 127). Here, then, is a new way of expressing the familiar transformation of words into things, a satirical metaphor that locates the source and end of all language in the organs of digestion and secretion.

Such a view of the sources of language cries out for psychoanalytic interpretation, and Norman O. Brown's description of Swift's "excremental vision" seems peculiarly apropos, as does Phyllis Greenacre's observation that Swift's satires reveal a "kind of linking of the written or printed word with excretory functions."[39] Swift has been the major beneficiary of such Freudian analysis, but one cannot overlook Pope's own fascination with the imagery of things impure. One thinks of the pissing contests in the *Dunciad* (equating literary and excretory competence, perhaps), of "Fame's posterior trumpet" (4:71), and the "brown dishonors" (2:108) of Curll's face. If it is fair to describe such a view of the world as neurotic, then both Pope and Swift share the same neurosis. In *Peri Bathous* literary language is treated as the excrement of the dull when Scriblerus confesses that "there is hardly any human Creature past Childhood, but at one time or other has had some Poetical Evacuation, and no question was much the better for it in his Health" (p. 13). There is no denying the presence of this excremental vision in Scriblerian satire, yet I suspect that Pope and Swift are less preoccupied with excrement per se than with human physiology in general and its relationship to creativity and consciousness. Consistently one encounters metaphors that equate words with bile, phlegm, blood, and pus, all natural products of the body; or with those foreign substances, like the magical elixir of the *Tale,* which may be ingested, digested, and circulated through the body itself. In short, the Scriblerians often treat the language of the dull as if it were the product not of intellectual faculties or imagination but of their grosser physical apparatus.

In the *Dunciad,* for example, Cibber's bathetic poetry is described as blood—"All nonsense thus, of old or modern date, / Shall in thee centre, from thee circulate" (3:59–60)—or as embryo and abortion, all metaphors suggesting the physiological sources of bad poetry. In *Gulliver's Travels* the origins of words are traced to the lungs, and the projectors of Lagado warn against using them, "for it is plain that every Word we speak is in some Degree a Diminution of our Lungs by Corrosion; and consequently contributes to the short'ning of our Lives" (p. 185). This argument, that words are but secretions of the body, is even more trenchantly expressed in *Peri Bathous,* where the springs of poetry are located in a "discharge of the peccant Humour, in exceeding purulent Metre" (p. 13), while the modern mania for writing poetry, the "scribbling itch," is literalized as *"Pruritus, the Titillation of the Generative Faculty of the Brain" (p. 13).* Perhaps nowhere, however, is this strange connection between language and the body made more forcefully than in Scriblerus's remark that no writer, however inept, should be prevented from writing because *"Poetry is a natural or morbid Secretion from the Brain.* As I would not suddenly stop a Cold in the Head, or dry up my Neighbor's Issue, I would as little hinder him from necessary writing" (p. 12), an assertion that ironically unites the excremental vision with the mechanical linguistics of Scriblerian satire.

Within the context of modern literary theory this emphasis on the somatic qualities of language puts one in mind of the complex theories of Jacques Lacan, who has argued that language is a kind of body. "The Word is in fact a gift of Language," writes Lacan, "and Language is not immaterial. It is a subtle body, but body it is."[40] But perhaps an even closer parallel might be drawn between Scriblerus's description of the sheer relief to be derived from "necessary writing" and that "erotics of reading" outlined in Roland Barthes's *The Pleasure of the Text*.[41] One thinks back to Swift's description of the critics in the pit devouring words when Barthes speaks of being "gorged with language," and it is almost as if Barthes derives a peculiar pleasure in taking seriously those ambiguous metaphors that in an inverted context amused the Scriblerians. Thus he speaks of an orgasmic "jouissance" that is transferred from writer to reader, of texts that "desire" the reader, and of the "certain body" of the text itself.[42] It is perhaps a measure of how radically our view of language has changed that Scriblerian metaphors forged in a spirit of enlightened lunacy should now be interpreted as wisdom for the age.

This connection between the word and the body in Scriblerian satire extends even to the ironic discussion of the origins of language in the brain itself. In the *Discourse Concerning the Mechanical Operation of the Spirit*, the brain is depicted as a "Crowd of little Animals" with sharp teeth and claws all clinging together with bees in a swarm:

> All invention is formed by the Morsure of two or more of these Animals, upon certain capillary Nerves. . . . If the Morsure be Hexagonal it produces Poetry; the circular gives Eloquence; If the Bite hath been Conical, the Person whose Nerve is so affected shall be disposed to write upon Politicks. [P. 277]

Here Swift's antimechanist satire arises from his exploitation of a crazed version of Cartesian physiology (capillary nerves) and the Epicurean idea that all atoms cling together by means of tiny hooks to form larger compounds. In the *Memoirs* one finds a similar discussion of the origins of words in a mock "treatise of syllogisms." Conradus Crambe, Scriblerus's tutor, describes how words are produced in a philosopher's brain where "Ideas rang'd like animals," where the major premise is "the male, the *Minor* the female, which copulate by the Middle Term and engender Conclusions" (p. 121). Crambe then proceeds to examine all the possible progeny that might spring from such couplings—legitimate heirs, bastards, abortions, and even a "*barren imagination*" (p. 122). The puns are legion here and they are at least vaguely reminiscent of the wordplay so characteristic of deconstructionist critics who treat words as though they were generated solely from other words, for whom words alone are the subject of study, the only "things" with which theory contends, all other considerations having been banished from the system. One is reminded of a theory like that of Julia Kristeva, whose notion of a "geno-text" from which other texts are produced seems not unlike Crambe's copulating premises that breed new words out of themselves.[43] And not unlike a number of deconstructionist critics, Crambe's addiction to verbal games and uninhibited wordplay finally renders him unintelligible.

In either case, whether they describe the processes of the imagination as the antics of little animals or as the amatory behavior of logical premises, the Scriblerians reveal a common resistance to the idea that speech and reason may be traced to purely physiological origins. In the topsy-turvy world of Scriblerian satire, it is not the soul, not that "God within the mind" celebrated in the *Essay on Man*,[44] which is the focus of attention, but the head and the brain. This phrenological fascination with the relationship between the outer shape of the head, the inner contours of the brain, and the functions of the imagination prevails throughout *A Tale of a Tub*, where madness is defined as the overturning of the brain, the shaking of the intellectuals, the literal dislocation of the cranial organ itself. The pattern recurs in so unlikely a work as *Three Hours after Marriage*, the farce jointly written by Pope, Gay, and Arbuthnot, where the hero, Dr. Fossile, attempts to account for his niece's penchant for poetry: "Alas," he concludes, "the poor Girl has a Procidence of the Pineal Gland, which has occasioned a Rupture of her Understanding. . . . Instead of Puddings, she makes Pastorals."[45] One finds more familiar examples of this phrenological metaphor in the *Dunciad*, where Pope draws attention to the peculiar "weight of skull" (2:315) and "impulsive gravity of head" (4:77) that characterize the Dunces. But perhaps the best description of the relationship between brain physiology and the creation of dull poetry may be found in *Peri Bathous*, where Scriblerus insists that all figures of speech "be so turned, as to manifest that intricate and wonderful *Cast* of *Head* which distinguishes all writers of this Genius; or (as I may say) to refer exactly the *Mold* in which they were formed, in all its *Inequalities, Cavities, Obliquities,* odd *Crannies* and *Distortions*" (p. 44).

The Scriblerians' interest in the whole question of the physiology of mind is extraordinary indeed. In the *Memoirs* they devote an entire chapter to the satirical treatment of Cartesian theories locating the seat of the soul in the pineal gland and corollary suggestions that moral choice and will might only be products of biological mechanism. That the soul should be identified with matter and mechanism was an abhorrent prospect both to Pope and to Swift. In one of his earliest poems, the "Ode to the Athenian Society" (1694), Swift complains of the "new Modish System of reducing all to sense," and throughout their subsequent works the Scriblerians are adamant in their hostility to the suggestion that man's most characteristic attributes, reason and speech, should ever be reduced to the clicking of gears or the swish of cerebral plumbing. Yet one suspects that they would not have been surprised that following the lead of Descartes modern science has accepted the biochemical model as one explanation for the origins of language. Whether, as Chomsky suggests, linguistic universals are a "biological property of the human mind,"[46] or, as Piaget argues, "sensorimotor intelligence prepares the semiotic function in general,"[47] one is left with the conclusion that at least in terms of its origins in the chemistry of the brain, the word is finally a thing. For us there is nothing shocking about Robert Scholes's matter-of-fact description of the origins of great poetry: "It is as if the poet in the process of making a true poem turns on some additional neural circuitry."[48]

Of course, such profound developments in our view of language can always be traced to more humble beginnings. For the Scriblerians, they could be traced at least in part to Thomas Sprat, or to those modern scientists and philosophers for whom he seemed to speak. For Pope and Swift, the reduction of words to things was an initial step in the complete redefinition of man's nature and his place in the world, and their concern for the fate of language has to some degree proved perennial. As George Steiner so eloquently observes, "much of the best that we have known of man, much of that which relates to the human, the humane . . . has been immediately related to the miracle of speech. Humanity and that miracle are or have been hitherto indivisible. Should language lose an appreciable measure of its dynamism, man will, in some way, be less man, less himself."[49] It is a function of their antiquity that much of what the Scriblerians found to ridicule has now become commonplace in our view of language, but it is a sign of their modernity that their anxiety for the fate of language and the future of English literature seems as urgent now as it did two and half centuries ago.

1. See Richard Foster Jones, "Science and English Prose Style in the Third Quarter of the Seventeenth Century," in *The Seventeenth Century: Studies in the History of English Thought and Literature from Bacon to Pope* (Stanford, Calif.: Stanford University Press, 1951), p. 109; also A. C. Howell, "*Res et Verba:* Words and Things," *Journal of English Literary History* 13 (1946): 131–42.

2. Thomas Sprat, *The History of the Royal Society* (1667), ed. Jackson I. Cope and Harold W. Jones (St. Louis, Mo.: Washington University Press, 1958), p. 113. Before Sprat, of course, Bacon had also argued the "first distemper of learning" comes when "men study words and not matter . . . for words are but the images of matter." Quoted in Howell, "*Res et Verba.*"

3. See Francis Christensen, "John Wilkins and the Royal Society's Reform of Prose," *Modern Language Quarterly* 7 (1946): 179–87, 279–90.

4. According to Warburton, the Scriblerus Club "projected to write a satire, in conjunction on the abuses of human learning," a program which I take to be a unifying feature of a whole body of satirical works including *Peri Bathous, Three Hours after Marriage, Gulliver's Travels* (Book 3), the *Dunciad,* and the *Memoirs of Martinus Scriblerus.* Because they also attack abuses in learning and because they are clearly models for most of the satirical techniques in the works above, I also include Swift's *Battle of the Books, A Tale of a Tub,* and the *Discourse Concerning the Mechanical Operation of the Spirit.*

5. Jonathan Swift, *A Proposal for Correcting the English Tongue, Polite Conversation, Etc.,* ed. Herbert Davis (Oxford: Blackwell, 1957). See also Hugh Sykes Davies, "Irony and the English Tongue," in *The World of Jonathan Swift: Essays for the Tercentenary,* ed. Brian Vickers (Oxford: Blackwell, 1968), pp. 129–53. Davies suggests that there is a good deal more system to Swift's linguistic ideas than I have allowed for here.

6. As Jones points out, there were grounds for such fears, for underlying the program of linguistic reform articulated by Sprat was an implicit materialism. See Jones, "Science and English Prose Style," p. 109; also "Science and Language in England in the Mid-Seventeenth Century," in *The Seventeenth Century,* pp. 146–51.

7. On the development of this view of language as representation, see Michel Foucault, *The Order of Things* (New York: Pantheon Books, 1970), pp. 42–44.

8. George Steiner, *Extraterritorial: Papers on Literature and the Language Revolution* (New York: Atheneum, 1971), p. 75. On the significance of the analogy between the Divine fiat and the spoken word, see Martin C. Battestin, *The Providence of Wit* (Oxford: Clarendon Press, 1974), pp. 79ff.

9. Steiner, *Extraterritorial,* p. 63.

10. Jonathan Swift, *Gulliver's Travels,* ed. Herbert Davis (Oxford: Blackwell, 1965), p. 185. Further references are cited by page number in the text.

11. See Robert Scholes, *Structuralism in Literature: An Introduction* (New Haven, Conn.: Yale University Press, 1974), p. 173.

12. In "Swift's Use of Literalization as a Rhetorical Device," *PMLA* 82 (1967): 516–21, Maurice Quinlan defines a similar kind of literalization as "a type of ambivalence achieved by contrasting the metaphorical and literal significance of a term, in order to reveal an ironic disparity between the two meanings." In *Language and Reality in Swift's "Tale of a Tub"* (Columbus, Ohio: Ohio State University Press, 1979), pp. 10ff., Freder-

ick N. Smith argues that "like Wilkins and Locke, Swift urges a return to things as the proper source of knowledge," a view markedly different from the one argued here.

13. Abbie W. Beiman, "Concrete Poetry: A Study in Metaphor," *Visible Language* 8 (Summer 1974): 197–223.

14. Ibid., pp. 219–20.

15. Ibid., p. 206.

16. Ibid., pp. 198–99.

17. Gulliver also discovers that far from reducing controversy and opinion, consequences which Sprat had predicted would result when men dealt only with sense experience and not merely with words, the "reformed" language of the Laputans makes them more contentious than ever, "vehemently given to Opposition unless when they happen to be of the right Opinion, which is seldom their Case" (p. 163).

18. Hobbes, of course, had already attempted to produce a prose style imitative of Euclidian geometry, and John Wilkins's *Essay towards a Real Character and Philosophical Language* (1668) had attempted to devise a language system based on a mathematical model.

19. C. P. Snow, *The Two Cultures and a Second Look* (Cambridge: Cambridge University Press, 1969).

20. Claude Lévi-Strauss, "The Structural Study of Myth," in *Structural Anthropology*, trans. Claire Jacobson and Brooke Grundfest Schoepf (Garden City, N.Y.: Anchor Books, 1967), pp. 209–10.

21. For a summary of Greimas's argument see Jonathan Culler, *Structuralist Poetics* (Ithaca, N.Y.: Cornell University Press, 1975), pp. 75–95.

22. Scholes, *Structuralism in Literature*, pp. 50–58.

23. Roland Barthes, *Elements of Semiology*, trans. Annette Lavers and Colin Smith (New York: Hill and Wang, 1968), p. 9.

24. Jonathan Swift, *A Tale of a Tub*, ed. A. C. Guthkelch and D. Nicol Smith, 2d ed. (Oxford: Clarendon Press, 1958), p. 60. All references to the *Tale* and the *Discourse Concerning the Mechanical Operation of the Spirit* are taken from this edition and cited by page number in the text.

25. According to Swift, he had read Lucretius three times during the year 1696–97 (Guthkelch-Nicol Smith, p. lvi), and Lucretian allusion figures heavily in the *Tale*. Generally speaking, when Swift attacked Lucretius, he also implicated Hobbes as well, both of them articulating a purely sensationalist theory of speech and hearing. For a more complete review of Scriblerian satire on materialism, see my "Metamorphosis and Mechanism: Aspects of Scriblerian Satire," Ph.D. diss., University of Virginia, 1979.

26. Roman Jakobson and Claude Lévi-Strauss, "Charles Baudelaire's 'Les Chats,'" in *The Structuralists from Marx to Lévi-Strauss*, ed. Richard and Fernande DeGeorge (Garden City, N.Y.: Anchor Books, 1972), pp. 132–35.

27. On the treatment of scientific metaphor as antimechanist joke, see Donald Davie, *The Language of Science and the Language of Literature 1700–1740* (New York: Sheed and Ward, 1963), pp. 21–40.

28. Alexander Pope, *The Dunciad*, ed. James Sutherland (New Haven, Conn.: Yale University Press, 1963), 1:65. All quotations are taken from the "B" text (1743) and are cited by book and line numbers in the text. Howard Erskine-Hill, *Pope: "The Dunciad"* (London: Edward Arnold, 1972), p. 45, speaks of Cibber as a "mindless materialist" and of the "physicalisation of thought" revealed in this image.

29. Aubrey L. Williams, *Pope's "Dunciad": A Study of Its Meaning* (1955; reprint ed., Hamden, Conn.: Archon Books, 1968), pp. 114–15. Williams writes that "in the catch phrase of the period, *res et verba*, one detects a steady shift from *res* meaning all subject matter—including the world of spirit and ideas—to *res* meaning physical thing."

30. Scholes, *Structuralism in Literature*, p. 31.

31. The concept of the materiality of the text is a fairly common one, but for two examples of its use see Scholes, ibid., p. 70, and Culler, *Structuralist Poetics*, p. 249.

32. John Vernon, *Poetry and the Body* (Urbana, Ill.: University of Illinois Press, 1979), p. 32.

33. Norbert Wiener, *The Human Use of Human Beings: Cybernetics and Society* (Garden City, N.Y.: Doubleday Anchor Books, 1954), p. 79. Robert Scholes speaks of Joyce's "cybernetic" theory of fiction.

34. *Memoirs of the Extraordinary Life, Works and Discoveries of Martinus Scriblerus*, ed. Charles Kerby-Miller (New Haven, Conn.: Yale University Press, 1950), p. 141. All further references are cited by page number in the text.

35. Beiman, "Concrete Poetry," p. 217.

36. *The Art of Sinking in Poetry: Martinus Scriblerus' ΠΕΡΙ ΒΑΘΟΙΣ*, ed. Edna Leake Steeves (New York: King's Crown Press, 1952), p. 36. All further references are cited by page number in the text.

37. In *Peri Bathous*, Scriblerus also recommends the construction of a "*Rhetorical Chest of Drawers*" (p. 74) with stops and registers much like those of an organ.

38. Marshall McLuhan, *The Gutenberg Galaxy: The Making of Typographic Man* (1962; reprint ed., New York: Signet, 1969), pp. 304–15. McLuhan notes the centrality of the whole question of print culture in the *Dunciad*.

39. Quoted in Norman O. Brown, *Life against Death: The Psychoanalytic Meaning of History* (Middletown, Conn.: Wesleyan University Press, 1959), p. 198.

40. Jacques Lacan, *The Language of the Self: The Function of Language in Psychoanalysis*, trans. Anthony Wilden (Baltimore, Md.: Johns Hopkins Press, 1968), p. 64.

41. The phrase is from Richard Howard's introduction to Roland Barthes, *The Pleasure of the Text*, trans. Richard Miller (New York: Hill and Wang, 1975), p. viii.

42. Ibid., pp. 8, 27, 16.

43. Julia Kristeva, quoted in Culler, *Structuralist Poetics*, p. 250.

44. *Essay on Man*, 2:204.

45. *Three Hours after Marriage*, ed. Richard Morton and William M. Peterson (Painesville, Ohio: Lake Erie College Press, 1961), p. 7.

46. Quoted in Steiner, *Extraterritorial*, p. 68.

47. *Language and Learning: The Debate between Jean Piaget and Noam Chomsky*, ed. Massimo Piatelli-Palmarini (Cambridge, Mass.: Harvard University Press, 1980), p. 80.

48. Scholes, *Structuralism in Literature*, p. 29.

49. Steiner, *Extraterritorial*, p. 101.

Breakfast, Death, Feedback: Thomas Pynchon and the Technologies of Interpretation

Bruce Herzberg

Bentley College

I N Thomas Pynchon's short story "Entropy," a character named Callisto explains—referring to himself in the third person like his model Henry Adams—that "he found in entropy or the measure of disorganization for a closed system an adequate metaphor to apply to certain phenomena in his own world."[1] By the end of the story, though, it appears that Callisto's metaphor is inadequate or at least misapplied. He has sealed off his apartment to create what he thinks is an antientropic "enclave of regularity in the city's chaos" (p. 280). But instead of protecting him from external chaos, his self-induced closure invites the stagnation of energy and ideas that he fears. Callisto's self-consciousness about Henry Adams's influence on him, his scientific banter about the Gibbs and Boltzmann formulation of entropy, and his explicitness about the metaphorical extension of entropy into "his own world" may suggest that Callisto is Pynchon's voice in the story. But half of the story is about Meatball Mulligan, Callisto's foil. In another apartment in Callisto's building, Meatball is conducting a lease-breaking party. The party roars on in a flux of disorder and calm, openly interacting with the city that Callisto has shut out, while Callisto contemplates his failure and waits for "the final absence of all motion" (p. 292).

Callisto, on the one hand, may have enunciated and anticipated the condition toward which Meatball's party, the city, and even the universe ultimately tend. By closing his apartment, he may have accelerated the inevitable—the failure of exchange, the condition of total entropy. On the other hand, he may have erred in his understanding of entropy. After all, the sealed apartment was supposed to hold off entropy, not encourage it. If closure is a special circumstance—rather than the ordinary condition of things, as Callisto believes—then "the measure of disorganization in a closed system" simply does not apply to the world at large. Or at least it does not apply in the same way, as Callisto says, to "galaxy, engine, human being, culture, whatever" (p. 283). None of the systems named in this sweeping statement is "isolated" or closed. None is reproduced or reflected in Callisto's "enclave." Still, Callisto has created a system that is closed both in space and information, "proving" his premise by manifesting it, even to the point of its own breakdown. Self-referring systems are indeed affected by closed-system entropy. But Callisto's closure is an intentional denial of exchange. Such an intention can hardly be attributed to Meatball's party, let alone galaxies and cultures. The party should be a reminder that closure is not inevitable, that there can be disorder without breakdown. Indeed, Meatball does not even manage to break his lease, which *is* his intention.

While any informed commentary on "Entropy" must account for the scientific and metaphorical meaning of entropy, it is curiously inadequate and unsatisfactory to identify entropy as the structural metaphor of the story itself, as if the story were as closed and self-referring as Callisto in his apartment. In the light of Pynchon's later work, it is perhaps easier to see that "Entropy" satirizes the very rationality of Callisto's created world (and incidentally, that it satirizes the desire for self-referring texts). But even without reference to Pynchon's later fiction, it is stretching Callisto's metaphor a bit thin to make it subsume the marvelous extravagances of Meatball's half of the story. "Entropy" simply does not illustrate the notion of entropy that Callisto articulates within the story. Rather, the story "Entropy" is about entropy-as-knowledge: Callisto is victimized by his metaphor, and not, as he thinks, by entropy itself. "Entropy" exemplifies schematically the theme that Pynchon develops at length in his novels—the theme of science as a tool of interpretation. The scientific images in Pynchon's fiction ap pear as models for his characters' schemes and quests, not as structural keys to the shape of the fictions themselves.

It is difficult to characterize Pynchon's use of science because, from the very beginning, he treats science only in the context of its application as an interpretive model. Moreover, he shows that the act of interpretation is not limited to the search for pattern and meaning. Interpretation imposes pattern and meaning, and there are serious, funny, and fantastic consequences of imposing the powerful paradigms of science on human experience. Still, it is tempting to base interpretations of Pynchon's work on the "extraliterary" knowledge of science that he uses with such disarming ease, tempting for the same reasons that Callisto uses entropy as a metaphor for his own world. The orderliness of science seems to be a stay against confusion, chance, and uncertainty. And that is precisely the notion that Pynchon criticizes through Callisto, who means to hold off confusion by calling it entropy, subjecting it (or rather, himself) to his knowledge of science.

Most of Pynchon's characters are interpreters, and their models come from many fields of knowledge. Each field—Kabbalah or chemistry, Calvinism or psychology, literary criticism or ballistics—serves as an archive of images for a character or an organization whose intention is to name and suppress uncertainty. Most of the schemes for order and control develop on a far larger scale than Callisto's. The Yoyodyne Corporation, which figures in both *V.* and *The Crying of Lot 49,* and the vast rocket-cartel of *Gravity's Rainbow* extend their metaphors of order and disorder through powerful technologies, with devastating results for those cousins of Meatball Mulligan who find themselves outside the corporate enclaves of regularity. Unlike Callisto, who shatters only his own dreams by enacting his metaphor, the technologies of interpretation in the novels threaten to circumscribe vast realms of life within and without their boundaries. Pynchon shows that the elaboration of science is already the elaboration of a powerful metaphor in *The Crying of Lot 49,* where Oedipa Maas realizes that "the act of metaphor was a thrust at truth and a lie, depending upon where you were: inside, safe, or outside, lost."[2]

In *Gravity's Rainbow* especially, where he is most playful about the metaphoric power of science, Pynchon demystifies the metaphor even as he draws us into a world where the act of metaphor is an attempt to create a safe inside—where the

power of knowledge makes the world at once richer, more
mysterious, and more dangerous:

> Now there grows among all the rooms, replacing the night's old
> smoke, alcohol and sweat, the fragile, musaceous odor of Break-
> fast: flowery, permeating, surprising, more than the color of winter
> sunlight, taking over not so much through any brute pungency or
> volume as by the high intricacy to the weaving of its molecules,
> sharing the conjuror's secret by which—though it is not often
> Death is told so clearly to fuck off—the living genetic chains prove
> even labyrinthine enough to preserve some human face down ten
> or twenty generations . . . so the same assertion-through-structure
> allows this war morning's banana fragrance to meander, repossess,
> prevail. Is there any reason not to open every window, and let the
> kind scene blanket all Chelsea? As a spell, against falling objects.[3]

In London in the winter of 1944–45, Pirate Prentice's mad
Banana Breakfast ("banana omelets, banana sandwiches,
banana casseroles . . . banana croissants and banana kreplach,
and banana oatmeal and banana jam and banana bread") becomes a charm against mechanized death in the form of the V-
2 rocket bombs. Here, certainly, is a passage that shows how
science can be used metaphorically, the allusions to molecules
combined with images of magic, the smell of Breakfast compared to DNA. But Pynchon insists on a kind of literalness,
here and throughout *Gravity's Rainbow*. He subverts any simple
metaphorical reading of this passage by the range and depth of
his references. Where in this passage can we locate the point or
points of comparison?

The odor of Breakfast "grows among all the rooms," and
though the odor is fragile (and "musaceous": like bananas) it
replaces the "smoke, alcohol and sweat" of last night's dissipa-
tions. It does not replace these other smells by force—"not so
much through any brute pungency or volume," since the
banana odor is a fragile, growing thing—but "by the high intri-
cacy to the weaving of its molecules." The metaphor here is in
"weaving" rather than "molecules." Pynchon refers to the
banana-ester, the organic molecule that constitutes and carries
the banana odor. But how is it that the shape or construction of
the ester can take over, repossess, prevail? What is an "assertion-
through-structure"?

The banana-ester molecule shares "the conjuror's secret by
which . . . the living genetic chains . . . preserve some human
face" perhaps for many generations. Here is an important
point of comparison, though metaphor may not be the term to

describe it. The banana ester and DNA can perform the same magic trick, but the two molecules are not very different in kind. Both are organic molecules that have the marvelous power to transmit information. DNA exemplifies the identity of information and structure through the familiar idea of the information of heredity. Thus "assertion-through-structure" is a literal description of the DNA molecule's action. Its fragrance is the banana ester's message, its power to replace, to grow, to take over is "the same assertion-through-structure."

The comparison between DNA and the ester is one of degree, then, rather than of kind. Norbert Wiener defines organic molecules, in cybernetic terms, as mechanisms of communication and control: "Organism is opposed to chaos, to disintegration, to death, as message is to noise."[4] If the living genetic chains are "labyrinthine enough," their message will be preserved—more complex organization implying greater resistance to disruption. If disintegration and noise are held off, the molecule can "preserve some human face down ten or twenty generations." This may be exaggeration, but it is not metaphor. It is the extension of a high-probability phenomenon to the edges of possibility. In the same way, Pynchon is being "literal" when he says that "it is not often Death is told so clearly to fuck off." The personification is a clever step up from the information-structure identity: the literalness is in the very real probability that death or noise will disrupt the reiteration of DNA's magic trick.

Compared to DNA, an ester is not very complex. Still, the banana ester has a distinct effect when it appears at Breakfast. It replaces the signs of dissipation with its message of growth and nourishment. But when its action is projected out along the diminishing curve of its informational coherence, the ester's power over death falls off sharply. Will it work for all of Chelsea, "as a spell, against falling objects"?—against the V–2?

Of course not. There are necessary limits to the power of organic structures over the structures of chaos, disintegration, and death. The *structures* of chaos, disintegration, and death? Yes, of course, the V-2, which is the real oddity in this passage, not banana kreplach or magic molecules. The mechanical structure of the Rocket is a parody of the organic molecule's assertion-through-structure; it is a product of the knowledge of structure turned to technology in the service of waste and death. The Rocket is at the center of *Gravity's Rainbow*. The novel shows how the Rocket came to be, how its message of death is sent by the complex organizations of science, technology, history, politics, human desires, how it is an act of metaphor whose truth depends upon whether you are inside, safe, or outside, lost.

Pynchon is hardly "opposed" to either science or metaphor. Scientific discourse is as much a part of his style as figurative language. Science may be "special knowledge," but it is not privileged knowledge in Pynchon's work. For Callisto and others, science is a powerful metaphorical vehicle that lends the weight of its coherence to the imagistically clarified tenor. But Pynchon insists that the images of science have equivocal coherence, a power that can be selectively tapped, a message that can shift from "opposition to noise" to the source of noise. The Rocket, particularly, does more than symbolize the message/noise paradox. It is a historical, technological object that marks a boundary: on the one side, mechanical order with its message of death; on the other, the release of entropy that "stabilizes" life, closing it in the only way that it can be closed.

The Rocket's symbolic possibilities are worked out by the characters in *Gravity's Rainbow* for whom the Rocket is an obsession. For most of them, it is a Gnostic Center, a transcendental embodiment of perfect order, timeless and unchanging. The actual death and destruction that it causes, the real motives of the governments, corporations, and individuals who build and use the Rocket—all are swept away, reduced, or rationalized by the apparent fact that the Rocket "itself" proves that the universe is mechanically orderly. Pynchon's demystification proceeds by restoring the alienated context of irrational human desire which is expressed in rationalized systems—the desire for order that makes an unnatural stability the highest expression of human understanding. Like the other interpreters in Pynchon's fiction, the science-minded characters in *Gravity's Rainbow* search for a key concept that will give meaning to the universe. The criterion of judgment for the "key" is the extent to which it holds off entropy.

In *Gravity's Rainbow*, there are many such keys or, to use Thomas Kuhn's useful term, paradigms: Newtonian mechanics, Pavlovian psychology, statistical mechanics, quantum mechanics, organic chemistry, information theory, cybernetics, and their variants and expressions in technology. There are nonscientific paradigms that serve the same purpose and have the same mechanistic bias. *Gravity's Rainbow* is inhabited not only by scientists and engineers but also by positivistic historians, deterministic linguists, linguistic literary critics, spies, economists, salesmen, radicals, reactionaries, racists, and bureaucrats. For these characters, the world is, or is best understood as, a closed system, mechanically orderly, predictable, and controllable.

Pynchon shows how these paradigms serve as epistemological premises for explanation and action. A fixed belief in the orderliness of the universe is manifested as a desire for order and control. The desire for order may well be irrational. If so, then the construction of a rationalized system to pacify or stabilize experience is only a reflection of the paradoxical desire. Pynchon treats this theme at length in V. The Whole Sick Crew, for example, espouses the aesthetics of Catatonic Expressionism or "technique for the sake of technique."[5] But their reductive exercises are pale imitations of V. herself, who enacts in her own body the encroachment of mechanization upon life by replacing her living limbs and organs with fantastic prostheses. The scenes of V.'s appearances are imperial power struggles: the Fashoda crisis, the failed Herero uprising in German Southwest Africa, the suppression of Maltese independence. These struggles reappear in a more potent form in Gravity's Rainbow. In V., they are disturbing enough as geopolitical reverberations of the general malaise. They exemplify the institutionalized belief that mechanical order is an appropriate model for the conduct of human affairs. International politics and individual metaphysics merge in something like the Futurist aesthetic of technology: "War is beautiful because it initiates the dreamt-of metalization of the human body."[6]

In The Crying of Lot 49, the metaphor of Maxwell's Demon occupies the interface between order and entropy. The Demon presumably has no real substance and uses no energy, yet it keeps systems orderly. But as Oedipa discovers, all "self-sustaining" systems must have an energy source and an entropy sink. The metaphor of the Demon hides the waste of the system, disguises it as nonentity. In the back streets of San Francisco, Oedipa discovers the human waste that complements San Narciso's solipsistic order; in human deterioration and death she finds the props of mechanical coherence. The power of metaphors of order is to seduce us to the side of coherence and to rationalize the preference for order as mere acquiescence to universal laws.

Because of their desire to confirm the paradigmatic power of explanation, the characters in Gravity's Rainbow search for the link between the Rocket and their own systems of interpretation. Ned Pointsman instigates the novel's major plot by devising an experiment that will explain Tyrone Slothrop's apparent ability to predict the paths of the V-2 rockets. Pointsman is a Pavlovian psychologist, a believer in behavioral cause-and-effect. When he uncovers the causal relations between the statistically indeterminate pattern of rocket-strikes and Slothrop's "predictive" sexual activities, he thinks, "we'll have shown again the stone determinacy of everything, of every soul" (p. 86). His "again" is a wonderful observation: a paradigm is always already assumed to be universally true. Contradictions, then, appear to be aberrations only. In each of the novel's subplots, a similar scheme for confirming the absolute validity of a paradigm serves as the premise for an attempt to *create* the conditions predicted by the paradigm. For the Herero leader Enzian, the paradigm is a combination of Kabbalah and thermodynamics. For the industrial cartel headed by IG Farben, it is a combination of monopoly economics, organic chemistry, and parapsychology.

The Rocket seems to be the confirmation of all these schemes, and so the most powerfully confirmed paradigm of all may be the Newtonian rocket mechanics of the scientists who design and build the V-2. The solipsism of such a confirmation is invisible to its creators. The very idea of *creation* disappears in the "universal" quality of the paradigm. Pynchon cannily shows how important the absence of the category "creation" turns out to be when the effects of the Rocket need to be rationalized. The universal is necessarily inevitable, and the Rocket can appear to be an almost mystical manifestation of the paradigm, a "law" become physical. The same sort of rationalization makes a Pavlovian conditioning experiment seem to be a discovery, and hides the manipulative underpinnings of IG Farben's "organic" market.

Thomas Kuhn has shown the power of scientific paradigms to rationalize contradictions. Paradigms are embodied in information, machinery, and texts, which give concrete form to the system of beliefs represented by the paradigm, and by their very existence provide "empirical" evidence for the correctness of the paradigm.[7] Texts and technology, in short, reinforce the belief in orderly systems. Pynchon is historically accurate, then, when he shows how the V–2 rocket, a great technological achievement, confirmed for many the Newtonian model of the human universe. *Gravity's Rainbow* is an exploration and a critique of the obsession with universal orderliness that rationalizes the paradox of the Rocket. Pynchon's style is part of the critique, which helps to explain why a novel with so serious a subject is so exorbitantly funny. Any detail or image, like the smell of bananas, any event, like making breakfast, may be the occasion for a flight of Pynchon's extravagant imagination. His humor depends upon accident and incidental detail, upon the excesses that show the value of unpredictability, the very accidents that schemes of order humorlessly try to suppress. Pynchon's catalogues of funny foods—as in the Banana Breakfast or the Disgusting English Candy Drill, another highlight of the novel—or the junk on Tyrone Slothrop's desk, or the names of his characters—like Slothrop, the New Englander, or Slothrop's friend, Tantivy Mucker-Maffick, unmistakably British—show how excess depends upon order. The strangest of Pynchon's effects have a disturbing familiarity. Bergson's lesson on laughter applies here: Pynchon constantly shows us that becoming mechanical is funny, even when it is also deadly.

One of the great delights of the novel, indeed, is to recognize, in the midst of some bit of lunacy, an entirely accurate account of history or science. When Pynchon explains entropy or chemistry or calculus, it seems like another of his fantasies. When he explains that Kekulé dreamed the structure of benzene in the form of a serpent with its tail in its mouth or that the V-2 engineers observed rocket flights while standing at ground zero, readers may well feel that Pynchon is going too far. Yet these accounts are as historically correct as the descriptions of the characters' strange obsessions. The obsessions are paradigms, but the paradigms reflexively rationalize their own obsessive and irrational qualities.

Perhaps the most striking example of how the rationalization process works is Pynchon's portrayal of the way that the V-2 came to represent an ideal of orderliness. Part of Pynchon's genius as a novelist is his ability to show how the principles of scientific orderliness mesh with the characters' lives. His characters are obsessive, but not simply because of the irresistible lure of abstract ideas. Rather, the abstract ideas confirm or represent principles that seem to be embedded in their needs and desires, in their perceptions of the world's organization and their own places and functions within it. Paradigms represent necessity first and reason second; rationalization is the ex post facto process of making necessity reasonable. Finally, the process of rationalization seems to confirm even the necessity of the conditions that generated the paradigm. The Rocket is a powerful rationalizing force because it is the locus of convergence for so many desires and paradigms. The Rocket is exempt from the Versailles treaty's ban on German rearmament, so the Army supports its development. The cartel controlled by IG Farben, already committed to industrial and economic forms of control, provides the materials for the Rocket. And the scientists of the VfR—Verein für Raumschiffahrt, the Society for Space Travel—have been building a space ship: they need financial support to live and to pursue their dreams.

The rationalization proceeds slowly. As the Rocket develops, so does the power of the paradigm that it embodies. Eventually, the Rocket "itself" seems to rationalize the army's growing presence. For the engineer Franz Pökler, the army's "interference" is an attempt "to superimpose their lusts and bickerings on something that had its own vitality, a *technologique* they'd never begin to understand" (p. 401). The engineers are like rocket-priests, servitors of a higher interest than mundane power. Pökler's wife, Leni, tries to reassert the connection between mundane forces and Pökler's work on the Rocket, but only forces the engineer into a more extravagant priesthood:

> "They're using you to kill people," Leni told him, as clearly as she could. "That's their only job, and you're helping them."
> "We'll all use *it*, someday, to leave the earth. To transcend."
> She laughed. "Transcend" from Pökler?
> "Someday," honestly trying, "they won't have to kill. Borders won't mean anything. We'll have all outer space." [P. 400]

For Pökler and the engineers, the Rocket is an undeniably material manifestation of the closed-system, antientropic space that Callisto dreamed of. In its complex guidance system, the Rocket accounts for every contingency. It proves that science and technology can overcome chance: "Beyond simple steel erection, the Rocket was an entire system *won*, away from the feminine darkness, held against the entropies of lovable but scatterbrained Mother Nature" (p. 324). For the engineers, the Rocket's victory has the most literal—that is, thermodynamic and statistical—basis. But is the Rocket truly a triumph over entropy, or is it an open system, ultimately adding to the energy-destruction of the earth? The Rocket starts out as A-4—Aggregat Vier—a combination of things, an aggregate of theory and technology, of tests and tinkering, subject to the sudden and swift entropies of mechanical breakdown. But as it approaches success, it becomes V-2—Vergeltungswaffe Zwei, as Goebbels named it: the Vengeance Weapon. There is indeed a victory over entropy here: all of the entropy is relegated to the other end of gravity's rainbow, the Rocket's flight path.

The Rocket is a closed system to the extent that it is self-referring and self-contained. The engineers, too, are closed in a system that shrugs off "real-world" deviations. Creating an internal guidance system for the Rocket, they create a parallel system for themselves. After the war, another engineer, Horst Achtfaden, sets himself a similar task, this time self-consciously: "find a non-dimensional coefficient for yourself" (p. 452). The physics of the Rocket works that way, defining the world in ideal terms first, and accounting for deviations later:

> you use dimensionless coefficients: ratios of this to that—centimeters, grams, seconds neatly all cancelling out above and below. This allows you to use models, arrange an airflow to measure what you're interested in, and scale the results all the way up to reality, without running into too many unknowns, because these coefficients are good for *all* dimensions. [P. 453]

The most literal, mechanical interpretation of the paradigm is the most mystical and transcendental, the least worldly. Achtfaden tries to invoke the old magic, but the contingencies have shifted on him. He cannot find a "non-dimensional" coefficient for himself—"the parameters breed like mosquitos in the bayou, faster than he can knock them off. Hunger, compromise, money, paranoia, memory, comfort, guilt" (p. 453).

Guilt is the worst, and Achtfaden takes a stab at rationalizing that:

> he only worked with it up to the point where the air was too thin to make a difference. What it did after that was none of his responsibility. Ask Weichensteller, ask Flaum, and Fibel—they were the reentry people. Ask the guidance section, they pointed it where it was going. [P. 453]

The Rocket has modeled the engineers' behavior, reducing them to instruments of rationalization, tools of some "higher" power of closure and control. The Rocket's life is vampirish, rationalized, separated from the human action that it feeds on. The engineers become like the thing they build, embodiments of Feedback, self-referring systems, holding off the entropies of "scatterbrained Mother Nature."

With the Rocket, the engineers cross the interface (an important word in Pynchon's work, contradicting the ideas of boundaries and closure) between mechanical and organic forms of control. The rationalized machine is elevated over "scatterbrained"—entropic—nature. Pynchon never mentions Hitler, Nazism, or the Aryan ideal in *Gravity's Rainbow*. It is either a monstrous omission or an extraordinary triumph for a novel about World War II. Still, the Rocket is as clear a sign as genetic engineering that the goal of control over change, accident, mutation, variety, difference, and contingency means suppression, mechanism, and death. For an organic system, as Darwin explains and Wiener strikingly reiterates, randomness and freeplay are the keys to homeostasis or dynamic equilibrium, hence to orderly adaptation, to evolution, and to exchange with the environment.[8] For a mechanical system, freeplay and variety must be damped out: they are entropic, they mean dissipation, disintegration, and disequilibrium. But at the end of evolution, as in a system of perfect mechanical control, all chance is subordinated to the perfect mechanism. There will be no further need for adaptation. Time will fall away, as at the Gnostic Center . . . and life will merge with death.

Part of Pynchon's refutation of this horrible equation is to have characters criticize their own past actions from "the other side"—from beyond their own deaths. There are two chief speakers-from-death. One is Walter Rathenau, the "prophet and architect of the cartelized state" (p. 165), who renounces, in Pynchon's novel, the cartel economy that he encouraged in post-Versailles Germany. The other postmortem comes from Pökler's colleague Roland Feldspath. In a long and convoluted message, Feldspath connects the German economy, the cartel's efforts at economic control (that is, the attempt to close the market by cartelization), and the development of the Rocket as a corollary and possibly saving effort of the "Discipline of Control" (p. 238). Finally, his message is an account of the co-optation of the engineers through the mystique of the Rocket itself:

> So was the Rocket's terrible passage reduced, literally, to bourgeois terms, terms of an equation such as that elegant blend of philosophy and hardware, abstract change and hinged pivots of real metals which describes motion under the aspect of yaw control:

$$\theta \frac{d^2\phi}{dt^2} + \delta*\frac{d\phi}{dt} + \frac{\partial L}{\partial \alpha}(s_1 - s_2)\alpha = -\frac{\partial R}{\partial \beta}s_3\beta,$$

preserving, possessing, steering between Scylla and Charybdis the whole way to Brennschluss. If any of the young engineers saw correspondence between the deep conservatism of Feedback and the kinds of lives they were coming to lead *in the very process* of embracing it, it got lost, or disguised—none of them made the connections, at least not while alive: it took death to show it to Roland Feldspath, death with its very good chances for being Too Late, and a host of other souls feeling themselves, even now, Rocketlike, driving out toward the stone-blue lights of the Vacuum under a Control they cannot quite name . . . the illumination out here is surprisingly mild, mild as heavenly robes, a feeling of population and invisible force, fragments of "voices," glimpses into *another order of being.* [P. 239]

The Rocket's "terrible passage" becomes the neatly aesthetic gravity's rainbow, the embodiment of a flight path equation, its deviations damped into equilibrium "under the aspect of yaw control." Like the banana ester—the molecule that the Rocket's complex structure parodies—the Rocket preserves and possesses. Only the Rocket is "better" than the molecule, in its perfect alliance with death perhaps even better than the labyrinthine genetic chains of DNA—for it is less subject to chance and change. The Rocket's change is abstract: it is just calculus. And its deviations are matters of yaw control and statistical distributions. "If any of the young engineers saw correspondence between the deep conservatism of Feedback and the kinds of lives they were coming to lead *in the very process* of embracing it, it got lost, or disguised," or simply rationalized, as Pökler and Achtfaden rationalized it. The mechanism of the Rocket is fascinating, and the equations are elegant. It is impossible not to admire, in a passage such as this, Pynchon's evocation of that elegance and the power simply of knowing the equations. Just so, it is easy to see how the young engineers could rationalize the Rocket's purpose, the motives and intentions that turn the engineers themselves into human replicas of the Rocket, reducing their work to "bourgeois terms."[9]

Pynchon describes the Rocket's internal feedback system not in terms of yaw control, but by describing the mechanism that controlled Brennschluss or burning cut-off. The Rocket did not burn all its fuel. At a certain point along its path, the motor would shut down, after which the rocket would complete its parabola by following the path of an ordinary projectile. Thus, at Brennschluss, guidance was finished and the Rocket was a creature only of gravity. As a closed system, the Rocket could not measure its own airspeed or position relative to the earth. A radio system proved impracticable (Pynchon notes) and a simple timer too imprecise. The solution was an accelerometer, which could be programmed to control both flight angle and Brennschluss by abstracting velocity and position from acceleration.

The accelerometer is a surprisingly simple device that can perform integral calculus: it can double-integrate the Rocket's acceleration. "In the dynamic space of the living Rocket," Pynchon says, the double integral has a special meaning:

> To integrate here is to operate on a rate of change so that time falls away: change is stilled. . . . "Meters per second" will integrate to "meters." The moving vehicle is frozen, in space, to become architecture, and timeless. It was never launched. It will never fall.
>
> In the guidance, this is what happened: a little pendulum was kept centered by a magnetic field. During launch, pulling gs, the pendulum would swing aft, off center. It had a coil attached to it. When the coil moved through the magnetic field, electric current flowed in the coil. As the pendulum was pushed off center by the acceleration of launch, current would flow—the more acceleration, the more flow. So the Rocket, on its own side of the flight, sensed acceleration first. To get to distance from acceleration, the Rocket had to integrate twice. [P. 301]

Pynchon describes the machine in detail—coil, transformers, diode, tetrode, capacitors—a wonderful device to stop time and rationalize death. In order to determine the Brennschluss point, a final capacitor was charged up "to a level representing the distance to a particular point out in space":

> Brennschluss exactly here would make the Rocket go on to hit 1000 yards east of Waterloo Station. At the instant the charge (B_{iL}) accumulating in flight equaled the present charge (A_{iL}) on the other side, the capacitor discharged. A switch closed, fuel cut off, burning ended. The Rocket was on its own. [P. 301]

With so much else to think about, it is easy to lose or pass over "1000 yards east of Waterloo Station"—already a euphemism for the houses of Parliament.

It may well be Too Late, as Roland Feldspath "and a host of other souls feeling themselves, even now, Rocketlike" suspect, too late to be aware of "a Control they cannot quite name" and a terrible passage, for themselves as well as the Rocket.

The "terrible passage" from animate to inanimate has been Pynchon's persistent theme. The complex network of complicities in *Gravity's Rainbow* links science, industry, and bureaucracies in the Discipline of Control, and helps explain Pynchon's earlier and more schematic scientific themes. In "Entropy," then, Callisto's error is to understand entropy only mechanically, only as the law of inevitable breakdown—and further, to believe in the power of a metaphor to penetrate to the essential laws of the universe. Even if Callisto were correct about entropy, there is no compelling reason to adjust human life to the laws of the universe or even to the "ultimate" fate of the universe. Here, as in all his work, Pynchon suggests that life is an accident, an antientropic aberration in the universe. Conformity to universal laws is therefore deathlike rather than lifelike. In *Gravity's Rainbow* particularly, Pynchon dramatizes the power of human systems to advance the conditions of metaphors and paradigms like Callisto's, and thus to create a world out of an interpretive method.

1. Thomas Pynchon, "Entropy," *Kenyon Review* 22 (Spring 1960): 284. All other page references are in parentheses in the text.

2. Thomas Pynchon, *The Crying of Lot 49* (New York: Bantam Books, 1967), p. 95.

3. Thomas Pynchon, *Gravity's Rainbow* (New York: Viking Press, 1973), p. 10. All other page references are in parentheses in the text.

4. Norbert Wiener, *The Human Use of Human Beings* (1950; reprint ed., New York: Avon, 1967), p. 129.

5. Thomas Pynchon, *V.* (New York: Bantam Books, 1964), p. 277.

6. Emilio Marinetti, cited by Walter Benjamin in "The Work of Art in the Age of Mechanical Reproduction," *Illuminations,* trans. Harry Zohn (1955; reprint ed., New York: Harcourt, 1968), p. 243.

7. Thomas Kuhn, *The Structure of Scientific Revolutions,* 2d ed. (Chicago: University of Chicago Press, 1970).

8. Wiener, *The Human Use of Human Beings,* p. 130.

9. "What I'm designing may one day be used to kill millions of people. I don't care. That's not my responsibility. I'm given an interesting technological problem and I get enjoyment out of solving it"—from an interview in Daniel J. Kevles, *The Physicists: The History of a Scientific Community in Modern America* (New York: Vintage Books, 1979), p. 408, n. 4.

Odd Fizzles: Beckett and the Heavenly Sciences

Charles Krance

University of Chicago

Between him and his stars no doubt there was correspondence. . . .
He had been projected, larval and dark, on the sky of that
regrettable hour.

Murphy

imagination dead imagine. . . . at the same instance that the black is
reached.

"Imagination Dead Imagine"

There again in the end way amidst the verges a light in the grey two
white dwarfs.

Fizzle 8 ("For to end yet again")

IMAGINE, you take an enormous mass and shrink it down to nothing. A very disturbing idea," admits Jonathan Grindlay, astrophysicist at Harvard University.[1] Since the publication in 1961 of *Comment c'est,* his last novel-length prose work, Beckett's writings, progressively shorter and more compact, have been for the most part evenly divided between playlets and pieces of short prose. Over the last seventeen years, the pattern of Beckett's creative activity has been dichotomous. Already in 1955, during the interim between *L'Innommable* and *Comment c'est,* Beckett wrote the following to Alan Schneider: "If I don't get away by myself now and try to work, I'll explode, or implode. So I have retreated to my hole in the Marne mud and am struggling with a play."[2] In her biography, Deirdre Blair mentions that Beckett "could not be away from theater very long without sliding back into a depression and losing the mental equilibrium that had become so necessary if he were to continue writing" (p. 635).

Prose has represented, for Beckett, a path leading endlessly inward; with every additional segment of shrinking text, the silence toward which his writing inexorably and logically must lead lies, paradoxically, ever so much closer to the most immediate layer of his creative consciousness. Left unchecked, or at least unbalanced by the outward projections of his "dramaticules," Beckett's prose pieces would likely achieve such singular density that they would approach what has come to be known in mathematical and astrophysical terms as "catastrophic collapse."[3] This *collapse*, or as Beckett calls it, this *implosion*, seems to have been stayed, for almost two decades now, by the counterforces generated by his "struggles with plays."

Viewing Beckett's work in the light of such struggles is nothing new. As early as 1938, in fact, Beckett himself composed a three-page essay, one of his first in French, titled "Les Deux Besoins": a geometrically diagramed apologia that "art comes from the abandonment of the macrocosm for the pursuit of the microcosm"; in the same essay Beckett states that the artist, in his attempt,"is doomed to failure" and consequently to "the eternal struggle" of inward quest and outward projection (see Bair, pp. 294–95). What may, perhaps, lead to some interesting parallels and similarities with the processes involved in Beckett's recent writings are the recent theories in astronomy and astrophysics, those "heavenly sciences" that have nurtured the Beckettian imagination and have played such a significant role in his works ever since his days at Trinity College (see Bair, pp. 220; 688–89, note 22; and 371). I am referring especially to the fascinating theories, which date only from the early 1960s, concerning black holes, white dwarfs, and associated phenomena, all of which can be said to relate to eschatology on a galactic scale, dealing as they do with the death of giant stars.

The abundance of present scientific investigations and the write-ups both technical and popular concerning the existence and behavior of black holes is such that an article of this length could barely catalogue them.[4] It is widely known by now that a black hole, according to this new science, is "an assemblage of matter that has shrunk—more properly collapsed—to a state so extremely dense that it has become invisible, [and which] because of its density, would generate gravity in its vicinity of such extraordinary strength that no light—or anything else—could escape from it; any light rays coming near it would be irretriev-

ably drawn in.":"5 Another scientist describes this infinite shrinking process as matter "disappearing into its own navel.":"6 In
other words, a black hole is a dying star that by virtue of its self-
compression to the point of nonexistence has achieved its "singularity." In addition to the theory that black holes are galactic
vacuums which suck in everything, including time and space,
there are the equally absorbing theories concerning their
"weird opposites called white holes." Inasmuch as the matter
and energy absorbed by black holes may somehow reappear in
the form of white holes, the latter, while linked hypothetically
to their black counterparts, are believed to be "located elsewhere in space and time"; their activity, meanwhile, is described as "disgorg[ing] matter rather than consum[ing] it.":"7 As
some scientists suggest, not all matter that is subjected to the
gravitational pull of black holes necessarily undergoes the same
catastrophic collapse: "under special circumstances," we are
told, "matter might be conducted by a rapidly rotating black
hole through space and time via passages dubbed wormholes."
According to a purely hypothetical scenario, "because black
holes play relativistic tricks with time, a space traveler who entered one and came back via a wormhole might find himself
returning to his place of origin before he left it. Thus in theory
he could see himself as he was about to depart.":"8

Surely, to readers who are somewhat familiar with the Beckettian universe, it would seem that Beckett's typology[9] of being
and nothingness, with all of the tensions involved in keeping
these interdependent poles apart as long as time and space
allow, bears an uncanny resemblance to the astrodynamic principles postulated by the new science. A case could probably be
made for viewing all of Beckett's personae as a circular parade
of particles of matter, each endowed with consciousness, and
each awaiting the collapse of—or reabsorption into—the hole
from which it was originally expelled: "Through it who knows
yet another end beneath a cloudless sky same dark it earth and
sky of a last end if ever there had to be another absolutely had
to be"—as the narrative consciousness bemoans in the last sentence of "For to end yet again."[10]

Reason prevents us from proposing that the entire opus represents a microcosmic facsimile of the astrophysicists' reconstruction and deconstruction of the universe, from its explosive
beginnings to its implosive collapse. But it seems manifestly
clear that in the twilight of Beckett's recent works the very life's
breath of the opus is gravitating, compressing and contract-

ing—indeed rushing with renewed urgency and vigor, though with increasing inner resistance—toward Beckettian singularity. These processes become increasingly apparent after the publication of *Comment c'est*, whose title, as we know, contains the pun on the act of beginning a new creation. Thus, the ambivalent term *twilight* perhaps best describes this period, suggesting, at the same time, the approach of full night and the beginnings of a new day.

Let us cite a fairly recent example of Beckettian ambivalence evoked by the advent of singularity. Just as in the case of a black hole, where "the matter that formed the hole has long since disappeared, like Alice's Cheshire Cat, leaving behind only the disembodied grin of its gravity,"[11] so has Beckett projected the absence of his own material being in the image of the disembodied Mouth of *Not I*, whose voice projects a "vehement refusal to relinquish [the] third person,"[12] that is, to give in to its own singularity.[13] Another example offers itself, this time replete with tantalizing coincidence: the "120-word skit consisting of light and breathing, lasting thirty-five seconds," titled, quite simply, "Breath," which Beckett had composed for Kenneth Tynan's 1969 production of *Oh! Calcutta!* (see Bair, pp. 602–3). In an article on black holes that appeared in the 4 September 1978 issue of *Time* magazine, we are reminded that "in the popular lexicon, the term black hole once suggested only the legendary hellish cell[s] in Calcutta . . . [but that] now it has become an immediately recognizable catchword for a different kind of darkness."[14] And, in terms of what has been suggested above, concerning Beckett's resistance to achieve singularity, it is noteworthy that the rift which ensued between Beckett and Tynan as a result of Beckett's agreeing to contribute to *Oh! Calcutta!* was largely due to the fact that "of all the contributors, only he [Beckett] was identified" (Bair, p. 603).

The "vehement refusal" of *Not I*, which might be considered as being typical of the prevailing spirit of Beckett's recent works, might also be viewed as a reaction to a process that had begun as early as 1932. In "Dante and the Lobster," we bear witness to Beckett's Belacqua, who in the despair of his incomprehension caused by his being "stuck in the first of the canti in the moon" (referring to those of Dante's *Paradiso*, canto 2, in which Dante, contra Beatrice, attributes the moon's spots to rare and dense matter), slams shut his volume of the *Divine Comedy*, simultaneously sealing his fate in the ever-condensing, ever-gravitating, ever-absorbing textuality of Beckett's singular prose—from which he will nonetheless emerge, periodically, in one guise or another.

It might be advanced, at this point, that what prevents the Beckettian cosmos from ultimate collapse is the balance which exists between his prose and his drama. This calls to mind the principle that, in Beckett's words, the "maxima and minima of particular contraries are one and indifferent,"[15] which, in turn, ushers in the "equals-but-opposites" principle of astrophysics, whereby matter and antimatter coexist in ratios of normally symmetrical differences. Thus, for example, when it was observed by a Russian astronomer, in 1844, that Sirius, the sky's brightest star, enjoyed an irregular path, the deduction soon followed that "Sirius had an unseen companion [or 'white dwarf'], and that the two stars were circling each other as they flew through the void, 'held in each other's arms' by their mutual gravity."[16]

There exists another possible explanation for the fact that the Beckettian logos, in its undeniably "catastrophic" course, has still not been totally sucked into the plenum-void of its own contractions: and that is that Beckett's system of black holes has made provisions for that cosmic safety valve known as "wormholes," through which matter travels only to "reemerge in a different part of the universe."[17] By literary analogy, these wormholes would seem to describe the channels whereby the motifs, names, and other components of a given Beckettian text—be it prose or drama—find their way into its "equal-but-opposite" companion text: intrastellar transmutations that prevent total destruction of matter in the gaping wound of the black hole, on the one hand; and, on the other hand, intratextual correspondence—or as *How It Is* appropriately has it: "migration of slime-worms"[18]—which prevents the Beckettian logos from collapsing entirely in on itself.

In addition to the reemergence of motifs in various texts of the same opus (and it is in this sense that I use the term *intra* rather than *inter*textuality), any given text of Beckett will invariably contain elements of self-reference, as often as not in the form of puns. The most interesting of these, for our purposes, are what might be called invisible; that is, they are conceptual rather than verbal. Consider, for example, the reference to the star Sirius, in *Theatre II*.[19] In this play we see characters A and B, in their mutually supportive roles, circling about mute C, whose face is unseen by the audience, and whose career is limited by "a black future [and] unpardonable past" (p. 96). A and

B occupy two symmetrically arranged tables and chairs, each with a lamp plagued by "a faulty connection" (p. 91), while outside the invisible moon casts its mysterious light on a static world that A grudgingly discounts as so much "nucler combustion" and "organic waste" (pp. 94 and 100). (This whole process, incidentally, is strangely suggestive of the action of pulsars, the observation of which led, by deductive mathematics, to the discovery of black holes. These, by contrast, "are by their nature singularly, so to speak, uncommunicative.")[20] On the third page of the text of *Theatre II*, A, looking out the window, asks: "Is that Jupiter we see?" [. . .]—B: "No. It twinkles."—A: "What is it then?"—B: "No idea. Sirius," the entire exchange accompanied by the switching on and off of their respective lamps (pp. 85–86). Then, three pages later, B reads from the documents relating to C: "The last time I laid eyes on him . . . he was seated . . . doubled in two . . . his head sunk . . . he was merely scrutinizing, between his feet, a lump of dogshit. I moved it slightly with the tip of my umbrella and observed how his gaze followed the movement and fastened on the object in its new position. . . . I had not the heart to bid him the time of day . . . I simply slipped into his hip pocket a lottery ticket . . . silently wishing him the best of luck" (p. 89). Sirius, we recall, is also known as the Dog Star, in the constellation Canis Major. The gift of the lottery ticket, inspired by the sight of C gazing at a lump of dogshit, gives rise, in turn, to the pun on the superstition that stepping in dogshit brings good fortune. Without attempting to draw any philosophical conclusions from the juxtaposition of these various elements, the mere fact that they coexist in a textual space of such restricted dimension suggests something other than mere coincidence.[21] It would, in fact, seem that Beckett here is punning on the concept of puns. To what end, one might ask? A pun, by its very nature, is a kind of "faulty connection" between two or more words or ideas; meanings are made to coexist as equals-but-opposites by means of a kind of short-circuited logic.[22] In the paradigm that I have described above, the result of this kind of faulty connection is the correspondence between the Dog Star Sirius and the lump of dogshit, both, in turn, sharing the characteristic of being potential portents of fortune for C—whose only reason for being seems to be "to take care of the cat" (p. 86), whose miaows, in turn, threateningly announce a "Black future" (p. 97).

Such puns in Beckett's works appear on close examination to be more than mere tidbits of comic relief; instead, by the intricate web of cross-referential correspondence that they create, they provide the infrastructure of many of his writings with just that reinforcement necessary to prevent the threat of "sliding back into a depression and losing the mental equilibrium that [is] so necessary if he [is] to continue writing" (Bair, p. 635). The comic element in *Theatre II*, as in many of Beckett's writings, is provided by the fact that his protagonists are unaware of their own puns; indeed, it would seem that it is their very obliviousness to the mutiplicity of meanings in which they whirl about that allows them to keep their heads above water, so to speak, or in other words, to remain just on the safe side of the "event horizon," which is what scientists call the "point of no return" of black holes.[23]

Let us note, in passing, that a variant of the motif of faulty connections, causing lights to flash on and off, already appears in Beckett's first novel, *Murphy* (1938). Its protagonist, while engaged in a game of chess with Mr. Endon at the Magdalen Mental Mercy Seat, observes at one point:

> that Mr. Endon was missing. For quite some little time Mr. Endon had been drifting about the corridors, pressing here a light-switch and there an indicator, in a way that seemed haphazard but was in fact determined by an amental pattern as precise as any of those that governed his chess. . . . Beginning with the light turned off to begin with he had: lit, indicated, extinguished; lit, extinguished, indicated; indicated, lit, extinguished. Continuing then with the light turned on to begin with he had: extinguished, lit, indicated; extinguished, indicated, lit; indicated, extinguished and was seriously thinking of lighting when Murphy stayed his hand. [*Murphy*, pp. 246–47]

Seen in this permutational light, Murphy, who "began to see nothing, that colourlessness which is such a rare postnatal treat, being the absence (to abuse a nice distinction) not of *percipere* but of *percipi*" (p. 246), establishes a strikingly strange interdependency with Mr. Endon, who is prone to "lay back and [fix] his eyes on some object immeasurably remote, perhaps the famous ant on the sky of an airless world" (p. 248).

If, in the perspective of such light-motifs, we advance that Beckett is punning on the concept of the pun itself, it might very well be that the reason for this lies in the etymology of the term: to *pun* is a variant of the verb to *pound*, and its original meaning is that of compacting a substance. By punning on, or comically mistreating, the notion of the pun and by extension, that of the increasing compactness of his own writings, Beckett, in his undying efforts to keep going on, is wormholing new apertures in the cosmic yawn that awaits. As the narrator in *Murphy* had stated over forty years ago—echoing perhaps Joyce's yet unpublished *Finnegans Wake*, which "in 1939 . . . fell seemingly into a black hole"[24]—"What but an imperfect sense of humour could have made such a mess of chaos. In the beginning was the pun. And so on" (*Murphy*, p. 65).

*   *   *

And so I must move on because I am in danger of coinciding with myself, instead of striving forever beyond my frontiers.

Michael Brodsky, *Detour*

The longer he lives and so the further goes the smaller they grow.

"All Strange Away"

He should not collapse without at least the form of a struggle.

Murphy

In astrophysical terms, the reductio ad absurdum[25] of the condensation of matter and energy in stellar bodies leads, theoretically, to either of two results: the invisible black hole, on the one hand, or, on the other hand, its "equal-but-opposite," the "white hole." But there are in addition the portentous white dwarfs to reckon with. Robert Jasper, of NASA, describes white dwarfs as "specks left in the center of a dying star,"[26] with what looks like a thick halo of light surrounding it. Technically, the white dwarf is also a collapsed star, but one whose "superdense stuff"[27] retains its inner glow for as long as it requires to cool off, the fires within preventing further gravitational contraction, until that fateful day when no longer able to sustain itself it "explodes catastrophically" and becomes a "supernova."[28] At this stage, it "blows off so much material in its death throes that the remainder is not massive enough for total collapse."[29] The possibility that universal light and gravity, as well as their mathematically deduced offspring, time and space, are mere pawns in the cosmic chess game being played out between such invisible Black [K]nights and White Dwarfs—neither one of which can be discerned except by the manner in which its twin or binary star acts—appears awesome enough. Consider, however, the possibility advanced by some astrophysicists that when the game has reached the halfway mark, and that universal "expansion gives way to contraction, the 'arrow of time' will change direction. From the viewpoint of an observer outside the universe (although denied the ability to make such an observation), our lives would seem to begin with the grave and end in the womb. Yet to those inside the collapsing universe, time's arrow would appear normal. In that case we would have no way to know whether or not the collapse has already begun."[30] What dilemma, one may ask, could be more Beckettian?

According to the "big bang" theory of the creation of the universe, "cosmologists have seized upon the hypothesis . . . that the universe, confined by its own gravity, is destined to fall back together again, [and that therefore] we are living inside an incipient black hole from which, even now, no light can escape."[31] The titles alone of so many of Beckett's works easily evoke similar considerations: *All That Fall;* "The End"; "The Expelled"; *Endgame; The Lost Ones.* In "Imagination Dead Imagine," the "bard of the bitter end" (as Beckett has been called)[32] depicts, in the bat of an eye, the dilemma of one who contemplates his own demise: the opening and shutting of the eyelid, which periodically admits the illusory warmth of the light of day, absorbs it, indefinitely, and cools it in the storehouse of memory. On another plane, the eyesockets, and what goes on behind them, suggest a kinship, both with the sucking-in action of black holes and the inward fizzles of white dwarfs:

> Emptiness, silence, heat, whiteness, wait, the light goes down, all grows dark together . . . at the same instant that the black is reached, which may seem strange. Wait, more or less long, light and heat come back, all grows white and hot together . . . till the initial level is reached whence the fall began. . . . But whatever its uncertainties the return sooner or later to a temporary calm seems assured, for the moment, in the black dark or the great whiteness, with attendant temperature, world still proof against enduring tumult. Rediscovered miraculously after what absence in perfect voids it is no longer quite the same, from this point of view, but there is no other.[33]

If light and dark enjoy such a precarious balance in Beckett's works, that balance is made more and more urgent in light of the fact that, in Beckett's cosmology, there is no recall of a primal "big bang." Rather, everything that occupies his time and space takes place *in medias res;* beginnings and ends are merely arbitrary attempts to fix absolute values on the degrees of gravitational pulls to which the individual particles of matter or the isolated moments of consciousness are subjected in their flight through the void. Even in a text such as "The Expelled," the moment of expulsion itself is left to pure speculation, which of course provides for the fictional stuff of the narrative. With each successive text, however, there is less speculation about fictional beginnings and projected ends. Instead, the processes that have characterized Beckett's concerns, ever since the wormlike creatures of *How It Is,* seem to lie more in the domain of resistance to the binary pull itself. Fizzle 8 ("For to end yet again") begins, typically, on just such a tension: "For to end yet again skull alone in a dark place pent bowed on a board to begin" (*Fizzles,* p. 55). What characterizes the "dark place," that "last place of all in the dark the void" (p. 55), whence and wherein all is "to end yet again," is its remnant of glimmering light; that is, the energy which, produced by past glimmers, has made of this void anything but a perfect one: "Place of remains where once used to gleam in the dark on and off used to glimmer a remain. Remains of the days of the light of day never light so faint as theirs so pale. Thus then the skull makes to glimmer again in lieu of going out" (p. 55). The skull's having "to end yet again" while "glimmer[ing] again in lieu of going out" conjures up, simultaneously, the theme of spatial and temporal circularity, so familiar in Beckett's world. The conjunction of this sibling circularity is prepared, of course, by the adverbial "thus"; less obvious, perhaps, is the paradoxical signal, which is implicit in Beckett's choice of the expression *in lieu of,* that the light energy, though its visible source may be faint, exerts a powerful enough force to prevent total inward collapse and consequently total blackness. For the skull, which glimmers again *"in lieu of* going out," conjoins time and place in an indivisible singularity, an action which, paradoxically, defies the very concept of singularity.

Here again, in his typically punning fashion, Beckett seems to be reaching for that point in time and in space where explosion and implosion, or expulsion and impulsion, join hands. At the same time he persists to skirt dangerously the event horizon of creative imagination. It is both the "again"-ness of the glimmering (or, the rekindling of dwindling energy) and the constraint from "going out" (in both meanings of the expression, that is, exiting and losing all its light) that define the ultimate place or *lieu* of the Beckettian universe. The "skull alone," in its "sepulchral" silence, is thus, in the end—"like the lone climber we meet at the end of Beckett's *The Lost Ones*, the last to experience the large scale vision of ultimate 'chaosmos' "[34]—privy to the endless plot of undying glimmerings:

> Skull last place of all black void within without till all at once or by degrees at last this leaden dawn checked no sooner dawned. . . . There again in the end . . . two white dwarfs . . . linked by a litter . . . relay each other often so that turn about they backward lead the way. . . . It is the dung litter of laughable memory . . . [s]welling the sheet. . . . And dream of a way in a space with neither here nor there where all the footsteps ever fell can never fare nearer to anywhere nor from anywhere further away. [*Fizzles*, pp. 56–58, 60]

1. Quoted in "Those Baffling Black Holes," *Time*, 4 September 1978, p. 53.

2. Quoted in Deirdre Bair, *Samuel Beckett: A Biography* (New York: Harcourt Brace Jovanovich, 1978), p. 458. Subsequent references to this work will be cited in the text.

3. In "Those Baffling Black Holes" we read the following:

If Einstein's theory [of gravity] is correct, black holes are the natural consequences of the death of giant stars. In what astronomers call catastrophic gravitational collapse, most of the matter contained in such a dying star begins falling in toward the stellar center. If the conditions are right, the matter crushes together with such enormous force that it literally compresses itself out of existence. The star becomes what mathematicians call a "singularity."

4. In addition to the sources quoted in this article, see the following: Christopher T. Cunningham, "A Guided Tour of Spherical Black Holes," *The University of Chicago Reports: Division of the Physical Sciences* 21, no. 2 (Winter-Spring 1974): 2–3; Anne C. Roark, "Some Close Encounters with Science Courses," *The Chronicle of Higher Education*, 10 April 1978, pp. 10–11; Thornton Page, "Space, Time and Black Holes," *Centerpoint* 2, no. 3 (Autumn 1977): 26–29; I. S. Shklovskii and Carl Sagan, *Intelligent Life in the Universe* (New York: Dell, 1966).

5. Walter Sullivan, "A Hole in the Sky," *The New York Times Magazine*, 14 July 1974, p. 11.

6. According to Robert Jasper, of the National Aeronautics and Space Administration, who was interviewed by Hugh Downs on ABC Television's "Good Morning America," 6 September 1978.

7. "Those Baffling Black Holes," p. 54.

8. Ibid.

9. Perhaps the term *topology* might be more appropriate: "Topology is a branch of geometry concerned only with properties that remain the same regardless of how a figure is deformed in a continuous way." Martin Gardner, "The Charms of Catastrophe," *The New York Review of Books*, 15 June 1978, p. 30.

10. Samuel Beckett, *Fizzles* (New York: Grove Press, 1976), p. 61.

11. "Those Baffling Black Holes." In keeping with the spirit of this discussion, it is tempting to detect a pun in the comi-tragic coupling of this last phrase.

12. Samuel Beckett, *Ends and Odds* (New York: Grove Press, 1976), p. 14.

13. Among the more interesting effects of black holes is the interchange of time and space, "so that, like Alice's experience in *Through the Looking Glass*, it would be no more

possible to remain in one place than to stop the forward march of time in our world."
And, although anyone unfortunate enough to fall into a black hole would disintegrate,
"theoretically, his or her image would linger, ghostlike, on the outer fringes of the hole,
where light does not have quite enough energy to escape, preserving indefinitely the
last glimpse available to an outside observer." Walter Sullivan, "A Hole in the Sky."

14. "Those Baffling Black Holes," p. 53.

15. This is a notion that Beckett quite naturally embraced when in 1929 he discussed
Giordano Bruno's principle of identified contraries: see his essay, "Dante . . . Bruno.
Vico . . Joyce," in his *I can't go on, I'll go on: A Selection from Samuel Beckett's Work,* ed.
Richard W. Seaver (New York: Grove Press, 1976), pp. 105–26.

16. Sullivan, "A Hole in the Sky," p. 25.

17. "Those Baffling Black Holes," p. 54.

18. Samuel Beckett, *How It Is* (New York: Grove Press, 1964), p. 113.

19. *Ends and Odds,* p. 86. Subsequent references to this volume will be cited in the
text.

20. See "Those Baffling Black Holes," pp. 56 and 59.

21. For a detailed account of the role played by Sirius—"this 'absurd' star . . . which
defie[s] rational comprehension"—and other cosmological features in *Murphy,* see
Sighle Kennedy's fascinating book, *Murphy's Bed* (Lewisburg, Pa.: Bucknell University
Press, 1971), whose index and bibliography provide many invaluable references.

22. We are reminded of "the short circuit so earnestly desired by Neary, the glare of
pursuit and flight extinguished." Samuel Beckett, *Murphy* (New York: Grove Press,
1957), p. 29.

23. "Those Baffling Black Holes," p. 54.

24. David Hayman, "Some Writers in the Wake of the *Wake,*" *TriQuarterly,* no. 38
(Winter 1977), p. 4.

25. As Sir Arthur Eddington characterized the theory of collapsing stars, expounded
by Subrahamanyan Chandrasekhar; see Sullivan, "A Hole in the Sky," pp. 25–26.

26. See note 6.

27. Sullivan, "A Hole in the Sky," p. 25.

28. See Roger Penrose, "Black Holes," *Scientific American,* January-June 1972, pp.
38–46.

29. Sullivan, "A Hole in the Sky," p. 34.

30. Ibid., pp. 34–35.

31. Ibid., p. 34.

32. *Time,* 7 February 1977, p. 84.

33. Samuel Beckett, "Imagination Dead Imagine," in his *I can't go on, I'll go on,* pp.
551–53.

34. Enoch Brater, "Fragment and Beckett's Form in *That Time* and *Footfalls,*" *Journal
of Beckett Studies,* no. 2 (Summer 1977), p. 70.

Hawthorne's "Modern Psychology": Madness and Its Method in *The House of the Seven Gables*

Martin Karlow

University of Minnesota

I N the first chapter of *The House of the Seven Gables,* the author makes the following statement: "Modern psychology, it may be, will endeavor to reduce these alleged necromancies [i.e., the romance's plot] within a system, instead of rejecting them as altogether fabulous."[1] Frederick Crews, in his psychoanalytic study of Hawthorne, which uses the quotation as its epigraph, undertakes such a reduction.[2] What I wish to demonstrate, in contrast to Crews, is that one need not impose Freud on Hawthorne to reduce the romance to psychological coherence, because Hawthorne himself is consciously engaged in much the same enterprise of systematic reduction. If a modern psychological equivalent can be found for Hawthorne's already schematized plot, one can restore to Hawthorne more than a measure of the intelligence and creative control over his medium which a psychoanalytic reading—working as it does in terms of matters by definition unavailable to the writer— necessarily derogates. Thus, although I am concerned with the meaning of *The Seven Gables* in psychological terms, the focus of this essay is literary. It is to reveal Hawthorne's methodology in his second long romance.

I

In his preface to the romance, Hawthorne speaks with obvious displeasure on the subject of "some definite moral purpose at which [authors] profess to aim their works" (p. 2) and adds that the way a romance operates upon our minds is not by overt moral intention but by some hidden nonliteral undercurrent of meaning. "When romances do really teach anything, or produce any effective operation, it is usually through a far more subtle process than the ostensible one." I believe the controlling aesthetic and the compositional method of the romance are found in these words. We may take the "ostensible process" as referring to the surface events of the narrative (i.e., the conscious) and the "subtle process" as its reduced psychological meaning (i.e., the unconscious). The following passage from the text provides striking evidence that this kind of contrapuntal method is operating. Its subject is Clifford Pyncheon, the aged, debilitated, and semi-lunatic hero of the romance, whom Hawthorne persistently labels an "infant." Clifford's "mind," we are told,

> appeared to have lost its proper gripe and retentiveness. Twice or thrice, for example, during the sunny hours of the day, a water cart went along by the Pyncheon House, leaving a broad wake of moistened earth, instead of the white dust that had risen at a lady's lightest footfall; it was like a summer shower, which the city authorities had caught and tamed, and compelled it into the commonest routine of their convenience. With the water cart Clifford could never grow familiar; it always affected him with just the same surprise as at first. His mind took an apparently sharp impression from it, but lost the recollection of this perambulatory shower, before its next reappearance, as completely as did the street itself, along which the heat so quickly strewed white dust again. [P. 160]

There is a passage about Priscilla's purses in *The Blithedale Romance* that students get a great kick out of, since it seems to be, *un*consciously, a lengthy double entendre.[3] Whether Hawthorne was aware of his humor or not in that passage, I do not know, but it is safe to assume here, in the context of Clifford's "lost retentiveness" and the incessant parallels between him and an infant, the subliminal (and ludicrous) level is intended. Hawthorne is writing about the perils of toilet training (from the baby's point of view) and, if not the "profoundest wisdom," his "nonsense" is saying something important about the character

of Clifford.[4] The connection Hawthorne makes is made sub-
liminally, and, more important, this "latent" effect is held in a
kind of contrapuntal suspension close to, but below, the surface
of the text. This is because, unless "take[n] in precisely the
proper point of view," as a suggestion rather than an overt
statement, Hawthorne's passage would indeed be nonsense. We
are dealing with what Poe would call an "undercurrent" of
meaning knowingly buried in the prose. It is no wonder the
author was always making strictures against over-literal read-
ings of his works. He was neither being defensive nor afraid his
obsessions would be found out. He actually had something to
protect from over-literalization. Hence, in his preface to *The
Seven Gables* and its fear of "expos[ing] the romance to an in-
flexible and exceedingly dangerous species of criticism, by
bringing his fancy pictures almost into positive contact with the
realities of the moment" (p. 3), he is asking that we read with
the same serious playfulness in which he wrote. The *House of the
Seven Gables* is a macrocosmic version of the scene of Clifford
and the water cart.

II

A number of years ago, Austin Warren labeled the plot of
The Seven Gables an "unavoidable nuisance,"[5] but it can actually
be shown to be an elaborate, though somewhat mechanical,
psychomachia, and it is surprising that in the 125 years of the
romance's existence no one has put together the few clues and
pieces that Hawthorne provides.

The "modern psychology" which "reduce[s]" the "alleged
necromancies" of Hawthorne's plot "within a system" is found,
I believe, in R. D. Laing's *The Divided Self*, a well-known study of
schizophrenia. Laing sets up a dialectic between what he calls
the *true self* and the *false self*. Both selves, of course, are one, but,
because the "ontologically insecure" person has never *founded* a
self on the bedrock of trust and love in babyhood, he grows up
with no "firm sense of his own and other people's reality and
identity."[6] Laing traces the failure to infantile nurturing and
considers it a failure simply to acquire the sense of one's body as
one's own, of others as equally substantial, and a trust in the
reliability of natural processes, all the givens, in short, for beginning life as a human being at all. He represents what he calls
the *embodied self* schematically as

$$(\text{self}/\text{body}) \rightleftharpoons \text{other}$$

and the disembodied or ontologically insecure person as

$$\text{self} \rightleftharpoons (\text{body}/\text{other}).$$

The self, that is, the true self or mind, experiences its own body as not-me and lives a fantastic and volatilized existence divorced from its being-in-the-world of others. This depersonalized body is referred to as the domain of the false self. The latter is a defense the insecure person erects to protect his weak self from the anxieties of a dangerous world, a world that is always on the verge of "engulfing" his precarious identity. As Kierkegaard might say, it is a relation of the self to itself in which the self wills despairingly to be itself by not being itself. Because of this division, the individual never becomes fully real, always exists at a remove from the real. What he considers to be most essentially himself is a buried treasure (like the supposed deed to the Maine claims and fabulous wealth in *The Seven Gables*) locked in a safe behind a wall, and what covers the treasure is merely a specious person, a pretend man (like the painted image of the Pyncheon founding father which covers the deed). The history of such a person's existence is the sum total of the being and doing of the false self, what the world sees as opposed to what he knows himself "really" to be.

Laing suggests that the true self and the false self eventually develop a sadomasochistic relationship. The true self, which is ultimately not more than figment, a kind of delusion of possible grandeur (again resembling the Pyncheon Maine claims), since it never actualizes itself, comes to feel that the false self is encroaching further and further upon its precious vacuum of inner territory, that it is being persecuted by the false self. The anxiety that provoked the erection of a false self to begin with thereby comes to be associated with that very defense. Finally, in desperation, the individual may decide to right the wrong he has done and "'be himself' despite everything," (L, p. 147) or he may attempt to murder his false self. According to Laing, both these projects, if carried through, are likely to result in manifest psychosis.

A version of Laing's history of the divided self, I believe, is the modern psychological reduction—the system within the alleged necromancies—of Hawthorne's second romance and can be shown to generate its plot and justify its often maligned resolutions. Furthermore, in its central character, Clifford Pyncheon, the author develops a portrait of the artist as a schizophrenic—another reduction of creative process to

pathological process. In the following pages I propose to reduce and systematize both the plot and Clifford, and then look
at a second major character and artist figure, Holgrave. When
these projects are completed, it should be plain that *The Seven
Gables,* for all its sugarcoated bizarreness, is a highly contrived
and, on its own terms, successful piece of experimental fiction.

Hawthorne, like Laing, begins with the notion of the ontologically insecure person and the splits in his being that result from
his failure to lay the first and basic foundation necessary for the
infant self to grow. Hawthorne fictionalizes this infantile disas-
ter in terms of the building of the house (substitute "head" or
"body") of the seven gables in his first, historical-background
chapter. Apparently the land on which the house was built was
nefariously acquired by a Colonel Pyncheon from a Matthew
Maule. The former later framed the latter on witchcraft
charges, Maule's last words being the curse "God will give him
blood to drink!" (p. 8). On the very day the house was publicly
opened (born), Colonel Pyncheon was found dead, clots of
blood staining his ruff.

For the house of the seven gables in its infancy, as for the
hero of Hawthorne's "The Haunted Mind," there is "some error at the outset of life," a "fatality" and "evil influence," which
must be endured forever after. Clearly, we are dealing with the
"something, somehow like Original Sin" Melville singled out in
his famous piece on Hawthorne's Mosses.[7] The ontologically
insecure person feels he has no right to exist: the Pyncheons
have no right to the land on which the house is built. The very
existence (birth) of the house (self/body) is a usurpation that
brings guilt in its wake. We are not dealing with oedipal guilt,
but guilt that begins even earlier, guilt that is tied to the very act
of having been born at all. It is, therefore, not by accident that
Hawthorne has a child discover the body of the dead colonel:
"A little boy—the Colonel's grandchild, and the only human
being that ever dared to be familiar with him—now made his
way among the guests, and ran towards the seated figure; then
pausing halfway, he began to shriek with terror" (p. 15).

What I am suggesting is that the house of the seven gables is a
giant head or body, that its birth and traumatic early infancy is
the subject of chapter 1, and that the conflict between Pyncheon and Maule is the conflict between the Laingian false and
true selves. Hawthorne refers to the house as a head on the first
page: its facade is "like a human countenance" (p. 5); later, its

second story is called a "brow" (p. 28). Virtually the entire romance is generated by, and concerned with, the sadomasochistic relationship between two Pyncheons, Clifford and Jaffrey, the divided self of the book. One can establish the former as the true self and the latter as the false self, but this leaves out the Maule family. The answer to this problem is quite simple: Clifford Pyncheon is "secretly" a Maule. That is why Hepzibah exclaims "he never was a Pyncheon. They persecuted his mother in him" (p. 60). That is also why Hawthorne describes Clifford, who has been imprisoned for murder, as "the thirty years' prisoner" (p. 24) in one paragraph and in the following paragraph tells us that there has been no trace of a Maule in the actual world "for thirty years past" (p. 25). Clearly, we are meant to pick up the repetition of the number thirty as a clue to this identity between Clifford and the Maules. Finally, Clifford has been framed like the first Maule, and the perpetrator of the frame-up is the spit and image of the first Pyncheon.

Before I show how Clifford is the true self and Jaffrey the false self, the uncanny resemblance of Hawthorne and Laing should become clear if I reduce a bit of Hawthornian "nonsense," an "alleged necromancy," within Laing's system. Thirty years before the story begins, a man named Uncle Jaffrey decided that "it [was] imperative upon him, even at this late hour, to make restitution to Maule's posterity" (p. 23). In Laingian terms, we could say that the true self has decided to give up its false existence, to be it despite everything—to give the real (e)state to its true possessor. Uncle Jaffrey was attempting to make restitution to the real inhabitant of his body. As we know, however, this project entails the murdering of the false self, and since both selves are only one body, the self is literally committing suicide or murdering itself in the sense of going mad. Notice, therefore, that Hawthorne has an Uncle *Jaffrey* murdered (albeit accidentally), and he has him murdered, curiously enough, by someone named Cousin Jaffrey, the evil Jaffrey of the book's present. In other words, *the self murders the self.* To keep the counterpoint between romance plot and schizophrenic process intact, the (true) self should now go mad, be locked away in the living tomb-prison of psychosis. Hence, Cousin Jaffrey frames Clifford for the murder—the false self persecutes the true self—and the latter is relegated to a "living tomb" (p. 22) at the same time the Maules disappear from the contemporary world. If Hawthorne could have read Laing, the parallel could not be more striking.

It should now be plain why Clifford is characterized as an infant, for it was as an infant that he failed to be properly embodied, and it is at this stage of life that this unfortunate existence is stalled: "his life seemed to be standing still at a period little in advance of childhood, and to cluster all his reminiscences about that epoch; just as, after the torpor of a heavy blow, the sufferer's reviving consciousness goes back to the moment considerably behind the accident that stupefied him" (p. 170). The water-cart passage quoted above is actually quite revealing of his situation. Never having properly differentiated self from world, Clifford experiences the world (water cart) as images of himself thrown back at him. That is, he experiences his own bodily processes as "world" or "other" rather than "self." The reason the activities of the water cart (whose shower is tamed by the city authorities as the child's shower is tamed by parental authorities) disturb and baffle him is simply that he has never properly connected his body and its functions with his own self-determined activities. Clifford is disembodied, split into a virtually distinct mind and body. His mind is compared to the "forlorn inhabitant" of a "dark and ruinous mansion" (p. 105), his body. Instead of (self/body) = other, he experiences self = (body/other), and the reification, or false self, of the body/other is Jaffrey, his persecutor, a man the very sight of whom throws him into a state of abject panic and terror. Once again, Hawthorne's fictional necromancies are very close to Laing's psychological system.

Thus, the most salient characteristic of Hawthorne's descriptions of Jaffrey is his corporeality and, more imporant, that his body is a thing of the world, pure externality, a facade, almost a caricature, of conventionality. He is described at first as "large and portly" and less an individual than a type. With the words "no better model need be sought, nor could have been found, of a very high order of respectability" (p. 56), Hawthorne launches upon a description of his clothes, that aspect of a person which makes him most an object to be seen by others. Just as the false self acquires a kind of autonomous existence, Jaffrey's sartorial paraphernalia are said to be all but interchangeable with Jaffrey: "His gold-headed cane . . . had it chosen to take a walk by itself, would have been recognized anywhere as a tolerably adequate representative of its master." Jaffrey is without subjectivity: "This character—which showed itself so strikingly in everything about him, . . . went no deeper

than his station, habits of life, and external circumstances. . . .
He would have made a good and massive portrait" (pp. 56–57).

Like Laing's false self, Jaffrey is a stereotype, a one-
dimensional man, existing in order to maintain an "appearance
of perfect normality and adjustment" (L, p. 101). "Direct relationships with the world are the province of a false-self system,"
the province of the man of the world, Jaffrey, while the true
self "is occupied in phantasy and observation" (L, p. 94), like
Clifford, the man whose being is not in but beyond-the-world.
According to Laing, the true "self fears being engulfed by the
spread of" the false self (L, p. 100). Thus, Jaffrey is more than
once seen attempting to "forc[e] a passage" into "the inner
room" (p. 129) of the house ("inner room" being the territory
of the inner secret self). Clifford responds with the voice of "a
frightened infant": "Hepzibah, Hepzibah! . . . Go down on your
knees to him! Kiss his feet! Entreat him not to come in! Oh, let
him have mercy on me! Mercy! Mercy!" Clifford is terrified
because "the 'inner' secret self hates the characteristics of the
false self. It also fears it, because the assumption of an alien
identity is always experienced as a threat to its own" (L,
pp. 102–3). If Jaffrey wins entry into the inner room of the
house-head, Clifford will cease to exist.

If Jaffrey is pure object, Clifford is pure subject, pure in-
teriority without substance, a ghost (which he is often called).
Just as the ontologically insecure person feels he has no right to
exist, "there seemed no necessity for [Clifford's] having drawn
breath at all; the world never wanted him" (pp. 139–40). The
one occasion when he and his equally depersonalized sister,
Hepzibah, venture out into the real world, all the anxieties of
mere being that provoke the false self defense system engulf
them, and Clifford despairingly cries, "We are ghosts! *We have
no right among human beings*—no right anywhere" (p. 169; italics
mine). Clifford cannot relate to people as others, but rather
posits them as his own imagos, depersonalizing their bodies to
ward off anxiety much as he has depersonalized his own.
Therefore, for Clifford, "Phoebe was not an actual fact . . . but
[an] interpretation . . . [a] mere symbol, or lifelike picture"
(p. 142). His disembodiment and dehumanization have pro-
gressed so far that he can only be conscious of being real, of
having a body, when he is is feeling physical pain:

Frequently, there was a dim shadow of doubt in his eyes. "Take my hand, Phoebe," he would say, "and pinch it hard with your little fingers! Give me a rose, that I may press its thorns, and prove myself awake by the sharp touch of pain!" [Pp. 149–50]

Laing speaks of this same phenomenon in his patients as an

> attempt to experience real alive feelings . . . by subjecting oneself to intense pain or terror. Thus, one schizophrenic woman who was in the habit of stubbing out her cigarettes on the back of her hand, pressing her thumbs hard against her eyeballs, slowly tearing out her hair, etc., explained that she did such things in order to experience something "real." [L, p. 145]

Thus, when Clifford stands high above the world at "The Arched Window," he is seized with an impulse to plunge to his death in order to become a part of the "great centre of humanity" (p. 166). He must die and be born again to be simply an ordinary human.

A man like Clifford, whose world has shrunk and narrowed into dungeonlike solipsism (the thirty-year sentence of death-in-life), cannot properly love. Laing quotes Medard Boss, another existential psychiatrist, on the subject of the male schizophrenic's relation to women, and Boss's language is close to Hawthorne's:

> The first step in the process of increasing barrenness of his existence was that the woman lost her transparency, being a completely different, remote "foreign" pole of existence; she became "pale," a mirage," then she represented "undigestible food" and finally she dropped out of the frame of his world. [L, p. 146]

Hawthorne describes a similar "draining" of real substance in Clifford's inner world:

> this man—whose whole poor and impalpable enjoyment of existence heretofore, and until both his heart and fancy died within him, had been a dream; *whose images of women had more and more lost their warmth and substance, and been frozen, like the pictures of secluded artists, into the chillest ideality.*. . . [P. 140; italics mine]

Clifford could say, along with Laing's patient James, "reality recedes from me. Everything I touch, everything I think, everyone I meet, becomes unreal as soon as I approach" (L, p. 146).

The self of the schizophrenic, according to Laing, becomes "in large measure unreal and *dead*" (L, p. 144); the latter word, as the reader of *The Seven Gables* will readily recognize, is applied to Clifford any number of times. His return from prison is rendered as a return of the dead to life and as a movement from invisibility and sound without substance to a wasted and epicene semblance of corporeality. Before he is an actual presence in the romance, he is "the murmur of an unknown voice . . . unshaped sound (p. 95), an irregular respiration in an obscure corner of the room" (p. 96), "an indistinct shadow of human utterance" (p. 97). "The schizophrenic suffers the unceasing fear of becoming nothingness, of finding his self collapse totally" (L, p. 209). Clifford became nothingness, fell into a Blakean Ulro of nonentity, and is now, as it were, recongealing. The following words from *The Divided Self* are true of Clifford: "Realness and life may not any more be directly felt or experienced," but Laing is quick to add, "the sense of their possibility is not lost" (L, p. 144). Hawthorne assigns Phoebe the role of representing this possibility for Clifford. She stands for "all that he had lacked on earth brought warmly home to his conception" (p. 142), "what he required to bring him back into the breathing world" (p. 140).

Hawthorne and Laing are strikingly alike on another aspect of schizophrenic existence.

> The oral self . . . is empty and longs to be and dreads being filled up. But its orality is such that it can never be satiated by any amount of drinking, feeding, eating, chewing, swallowing. It is unable to incorporate anything. It remains a bottomless pit; a gaping maw that can never be filled up. [L, pp. 144–45]

Clifford's single "aggressive" activity is eating; indeed, he is positively voracious:

> [His smile] was followed by a coarser expression. . . . It was a look of appetite. He ate food with what might almost be termed voracity; and seemed to forget himself, Hepzibah, the young girl, and everything else around him, in the sensual enjoyment which the bountifully spread table afforded. . . .
> In a little while, the guest became sensible of the fragrance of the yet untasted coffee. He quaffed it eagerly. The subtle essence acted on him like a charmed draught, and caused the opaque substance of his animal being to grow transparent, or, at least, translucent. . . .
> "More, more!" he cried, with nervous haste in his utterance, as if anxious to retain his grasp of what sought to escape him. "This is what I need! Give me more!" [P. 107]

Clifford is hungry not simply for food; he is hungry for reality. So impoverished is his inner world that he has become a vacuum, never enriched by experience, but entrapped in a dungeon where the self relates only to itself. Laing writes: "The individual who may at one time have felt predominantly 'out-side' the life going on *there*, which he affects to despise as petty and commonplace compared to the richness he has *here*, inside himself now longs to get *inside* life again, and get life inside himself, so dreadful is his inner deadness" (L, p. 75). Thus, although Clifford feels "a shivering repugnance at the idea of personal contact with the world, a powerful impulse still seized on [him] whenever the rush and roar of the human tide grew strongly audible to him" (p. 165). Hawthorne underscores Clifford's "reality-hunger" by giving him a speech parallel to the food passage quoted above. Clifford is again crying for what he wants, but what he wants to incorporate is not food: "'I want my happiness!' at last he murmured, hoarsely and indistinctly, hardly shaping out the words. 'Many, many years have I waited for it! It is late! It is late! I want my happiness!'" (p. 157).

One other characteristic of the schizophrenic's mode of being deserves mention in relation to Clifford. According to Laing, the obverse of the schizophrenic's dread of relationship to another is rage against the other for the threat that simple relating poses for him (L, p. 52). The theft of Phoebe's subjectivity becomes a major issue in her relationship with Holgrave, but Clifford and Hepzibah, in their "clam-like dependency" (the words are Laing's) on the girl, also rob her of her vitality:

> A flower, for instance, as Phoebe herself observed, always began to droop sooner in Clifford's hand, or Hepzibah's, than in her own; and by the same law, converting her whole daily life into a flower fragrance for these two sickly spirits, the blooming girl must inevitably droop and fade much sooner than if worn on a younger and happier breast. [P. 174]

Though the gothic element is muted, Hawthorne's point is that Clifford, the man who not only eats to live but is starving for life itself, is a vampire. "Other people supply me with my existence," says one of Laing's patients (L, p. 52).

This issue is finally, and flatly, stated by Holgrave:

> "Whatever health, comfort, and natural life exists in the house is embodied in your person. . . . Miss Hepzibah, by secluding herself from society . . . is . . . dead. . . . Your poor cousin Clifford is another dead and long-buried person, on whom the governor and council have wrought a necromantic miracle. I should not wonder if he were to crumble away, some morning, after you are gone, and

nothing be seen of him more, except a heap of dust. . . . They both exist by you."[P. 216]

Holgrave is, in fact, largely correct, but his language needs to be explained in terms of Hawthorne's "subtile process." Clifford's growing love for, and trust in, Phoebe is, in clinical terms, the only possible way back for the schizophrenic, or, as Laing puts it, "the schizophrenic ceases to be schizophrenic when he meets someone by whom he feels understood" (L, p. 165). Phoebe, by treating Clifford as the needy infant he truly is, by indulging him, allows him the space requisite for him to "regress" to the period in his life when he experienced the "heavy blow . . . that stupefied him" (p. 170) in order to repair the damage and so begin a second time. She enacts the role, which the doctor enacts in cases of schizophrenia, of surrogate mother, providing the grounds for the establishment of the ontological security that the original mother failed to provide. Because of Phoebe, Clifford is "in a state of second growth and recovery" (p. 173). His regression is not a deterioration, but a long-delayed progression.

Ludwig Binswanger's analysis of where such an existence as Clifford's is lost and the conditions for its return is most enlightening in this respect. According to this "modern psychologist," the schizophrenic falls into the condition of Extravagance (Verstiegenheit).[8] He falls, as it were, or soars out of experience, wanders beyond the world of everyday cares into a place from which he is no longer able to descend. Binswanger compares this pathological symptom to a mountain climber who climbs beyond the limits of his self, becomes stalled on a precipice, and cannot come down unless rescued by outside help. The chapter entitled "The Arched Window" is as close an equivalent to this state as we are likely to find in literature, closer than Binswanger's own choice, Ibsen's The Master Builder. There, we find Clifford imprisoned above the ordinary world, the "human tide" (p. 165). His only mode of reentry is suicide: "he required to take a deep, deep plunge into the ocean of human life, and to sink down and be covered by its profoundness, and then to emerge, sobered, invigorated, restored to the world and to himself" (p. 166). But to plunge is to die: "he required nothing less than the great final remedy—death!" The only alternative is outside help, someone "to bring him back into the breathing world. Persons who have wandered . . . out of the common tract of things [i.e., become extra-vagant],[9] desire nothing so much as to

be led back. They shiver in their *loneliness . . . on a mountain*top"
(p. 140; italics mine). Clifford's existence is stalled in infancy;
he has climbed beyond what Binswanger calls his "breadth of
experience." Only a sense of home or community, a "renew[al]"
of "the broken links of brotherhood with his kind" (pp. 166–67)
will bring him back. It is precisely such "ontological security"
that Phoebe abundantly provides. She gives the aged infant
reality. Her "presence made a home about her—that very
sphere which the outcast . . . above [mankind] pines after—a
home! She was real! Holding her hand, you felt something . . .
and so long as you should feel its grasp . . . the world was no
longer a delusion" (pp. 140–41). At the romance's conclusion,
she will rescue Holgrave exactly the same way from precisely
the same condition.

If the subtle process of *The Seven Gables* is to continue its
contrapuntal, "invisible" sequence just below the level of plot,
the sequence of events that transpires when Phoebe departs
from the house of the seven gables requires explanation. Here,
too, one notices how readily Hawthorne's contrived "necromancies" translate into a Laingian model. We can accept as a
given the fact that Clifford's whole life is the product of "an
error" suffered "at the outset of life" which caused him to grow
up schizophrenic. If we can further accept the hypothesis that
people such as Clifford fail at the outset due to the inadequacy
of their mothers, Phoebe's departure is easily seen as a repetition of Clifford's primal loss. In order to maintain the parallel,
it is necessary that the anxiety attendant upon separation from
Phoebe, duplicating as it does Clifford's traumatic infantile experience (which, for the duration of the book, he has been
reexperiencing), be powerful enough to provoke psychosis.
The dreaded world should force a passage into the inner room
and engulf or impinge upon the fragile identity of the true self,
"imploding" it as gas rushing into a vacuum. So it is that with
Phoebe's departure Clifford is "cut off" (p. 223) and withdraws
into the depths of the inner room, "wrap[ping] himself in an
old cloak" (p. 224). And who should suddenly appear, ruthlessly determined to confront him, finally, in his protected inner sanctum, but Jaffrey Pyncheon. "I must see him" (p. 233),
says Jaffrey, as if compulsively forced to act his part, as if help-
lessly potentiated by the logic of the subtle process. Lest we
miss the point—that Hawthorne is again setting up the conditions for an outbreak of psychosis—Hepzibah attempts to drive

Jaffrey away with these words: "Never! It would drive him mad." Unless he is allowed entry, Jaffrey threatens to have Clifford committed to a lunatic asylum. The encroachments of the false self, once again, can no longer be withstood.

Of course what transpires during the confrontation between Clifford and Jaffrey is the reverse of the historical pattern: Jaffrey, not Clifford, dies. Yet, upon closer inspection, the conditions for the outbreak of madness are actually fulfilled—and this is explicitly stated by Hawthorne. Clifford, the true self, in "murdering" his false self in order to be himself once and for all, does go mad, but it is a special kind of madness. Hepzibah's first response when she sees him after the confrontation is a "dread that her stern kinsman's ominous visit had driven her poor brother to absolute insanity" (p. 249). On the "ostensible" level, the two old people flee the house, finally participating in the world in which their previous attempt had failed. They take a frantic, whirlwind train ride, which Hawthorne carefully describes more as a vertical/air than a horizontal/land journey, and return to the house, Clifford's momentary wild exhilaration subsiding back into depression. On the subtile level, I would suggest that Hawthorne's subject at this point is the conditions requisite for the functioning of his own creativity, a vertical rising, an afflatus in short, that the author feels partakes more of the demoniac than the divine, and which he himself *reduces* to a pathological entity. Clifford is quite literally carried up and away into a volatile world of inspiration, but Hawthorne himself gives us the right to label his experience, clinically, as a manic "flight of ideas" rather than an outburst of the creative imagination. In this regard, but parenthetically, it should be noticed that the author now fuses with Clifford, assumes his identity, so to speak. Before leaving the house, Clifford had stood on the threshold, pointing his finger at the dead Jaffrey, on his face "an expression of scorn and mockery" (p. 249). It is precisely these emotions that the author adopts in order to deliver the astonishing chapter-long diatribe against the dead judge, "Governor Pyncheon." Hawthorne here adopts the role of the true self and acts out a situation described by Laing as follows:

What is called psychosis is sometimes simply the sudden removal of the veil of the false self, [i.e., the death of Jaffrey], which had been serving to maintain an outer behavioural normality that may, long

ago, have failed to be any reflection of the state of affairs in the
secret self. Then the self will pour out accusations of persecution at
the hands of that person with whom the false self has been comply-
ing for years. [L, p. 100]

What I wish to make clear is that Clifford's airy train ride
(and, more specifically, the exalted mood he is in during it) is a
vol imaginaire, a Binswangerian "flight of ideas." Hawthorne
calls it a flight, too, and approximates Binswanger's terminology in calling Clifford's state an "intellectual dance" (p. 262)
and a "bubbling up-gush of ideas" (p. 266). "It not a little re-
sembled the exhilaration of wine" (p. 254). Like the imagination in reverie, Clifford transcends space and time: "The spires
of meeting houses seemed set adrift from their foundations;
the broad-based hills glided away. Everything was unfixed . . . "
(p. 256). Hawthorne characterizes "the wild effervescence of
his mood" (p. 266) as a temporary and diseased "high." Clifford
spouts a quasitranscendental theory of human perfectibility
and universal human love, all expressed with a comical idealism
bordering on what Kierkegaard calls "abstract sentimental-
ity."[10] In Binswanger's words, Clifford is "carried into the 'airy
heights' of (an) optimistic mood . . . without regard to experience." There is a disproportion "rooted in an excess of breadth
(of 'leaping') and of the heights of mere *vol imaginaire* that
outweigh the (authentic) heights of decision. It is rooted in the
excessive heights of decision that outweigh the breadth of experience."[11] (Thus Clifford utters prophetic nonsense, a social
theory which is wildly implausible.) Binswanger is speaking of
manic ideation, a psychological reduction of the state the liter-
ary-minded person would call *inspiration.* I quote Binswanger
on the subject rather than, say, Coleridge, because for Hawthorne, the anti-Romantic who happened to be cursed with a
disease called imagination, the *vol imaginaire* is abnormal, ultimately depleting, and most of all, *unnatural.* Clifford's flight is
called "an event that transcended ordinary rules" (p. 305).
"This flight," says Holgrave, "it distorts everything" (p. 304),
and, indeed, only *because* of his flight does Clifford fall under
suspicion of murdering Jaffrey. Such energy is finally destruc-
tive to the self who experiences it: "A powerful excitement had
given him energy and vivacity. Its operation over, he forthwith
began to sink" (p. 266). Clifford falls back into passive dependency: "'You must take the lead now, Hepzibah!' murmured
he, with a torpid and reluctant utterance. 'Do with me as you
will.'" Clifford's use for the *psychomachia* is now over, and the

romance turns to Holgrave. In terms of the subtile process, however, I will show that there is really no break in continuity. Clifford's vertical flight carries him into the state of *Extravagance,* but it is Holgrave whom we discover in this condition. In order to explain this necromancy, we must understand the meaning of Holgrave's relation to Clifford.[12]

III

If the theory I am presenting is valid, not only is Clifford schizophrenic, but the romance itself, of which he is the center, can be called an example of "schizophrenic form," insofar as its structure is seen to duplicate the Laingian model for the structure of the schizophrenic personality. I mean this in the sense that the book's ostensible plot and its explicit moral are pretexts—a false-self system—for the hidden or subtile process—the true self. Notice Hawthorne's virtual dismissal of "definite moral purpose" in his preface:

> Many writers lay very great stress upon some definite moral purpose, at which they profess to aim their works. *Not to be deficient in this particular,* the author has provided himself with a moral—the truth, namely, that the wrongdoing of one generation lives into the successive ones . . . however, . . . when romances do really teach anything, or produce any effective operation, it is usually through a far more subtile process than the ostensible one. *The author has considered it hardly worth his while,* therefore, relentlessly to impale the story with its moral as with an iron rod. . . . [P. 2; italics mine]

The relationship between the Hawthornian ostensible process and subtile process is analogous to the relationship between the Laingian false self and true self. *The House of the Seven Gables* may be compared to "the individual whose false-self system has remained intact and has not become devastated by attacks from the self . . . [he] may present the appearance of complete normality. However, *behind this sane façade* an interior psychotic process may be going on secretly and silently" (L, p. 147; italics mine). The latter phenomenon, I have been arguing, is going on behind the romance with its definite moral purpose. One might call this a curious wedding of content with form, a book about a schizophrenic, which itself participates in a schizophrenic mode of "behavior," but I do not intend this comparison perversely. Rather, I believe Hawthorne aimed precisely at this effect of a pleasant, ingratiatingly Dickensian and accessible facade with a seething, moiling depth of darkness secreted within. Most important to him was the fact that the precious hidden treasure be synchronized with the facade, that it should be continuous and, most of all, continuously *sustained,* as it were, in air, invisibly. Or, as Jaffrey (of all people) says of Clifford's storytelling, "He has the secret. [His words] had a backbone of solid meaning within the mystery of his expression" (p. 235). Jaffrey's words may stand as an artistic credo in this romance.

Until one final piece of the jig-saw puzzle is fitted into place, however, total coherence for the romance's plot and subtile process in the terms I have used to describe them cannot be claimed. This final piece is the book's oddly passive young hero, Holgrave, the daguerreotypist. Holgrave lodges at the seven gables; he is a young man of radical proclivities who meets and is drawn to Phoebe during her visit with her anxiety-ridden Aunt Hepzibah and Uncle Clifford. At one point Holgrave mesmerizes the maiden by reciting a legend about one of the earlier Pyncheons, Alice. Hawthorne views this act as a theft of the girl's subjectivity and allows the young artist to resist the temptation to enslave another's consciousness. At the end of the romance, we find Holgrave propped, strangely, beside the figure of the dead Jaffrey, stunned and paralyzed by the corpse. Phoebe rescues him from this shock simply by returning to the house and entering the room. The two, of course, will marry, but not until Holgrave reveals that his real name is Maule.

The question we must ask is, Where does Holgrave fit into the subtile process of the book? Certainly his marriage to Phoebe, she a Pyncheon, he a Maule, points toward a reintegration of the divided self. Also certain is the fact that Holgrave is another "true self figure," locked away in the back of the household, and that his adoption of his proper identity at the end means that the true self has finally become the *real* self and entered the world. Hawthorne establishes Holgrave's alienation by describing him as "a lodger in a remote gable—quite a house by itself, indeed—with locks, bolts, and oaken bars on all the intervening doors" (p. 30). Later, at the very moment when the confrontation between Clifford and Jaffrey is occurring off-stage, Hawthorne writes:

[Hepzibah] unbolted a door, cobwebbed and long disused, but which had served as a former *medium of communication* between her own part of the house and the gable where the wandering daguerreotypist had now established his temporary home. [P. 244; italics mine]

The clues seem to say that there is a connection between Clifford's sudden burst into manhood and mania and Holgrave's attainment of the Hawthornian sine qua non of "intercourse with the world" (9:6).

Holgrave and Clifford, it would follow, are *doubles*. Both are artists of sorts, and both have a basically detached and "oral" orientation toward the external world. "In [Holgrave's] relation with [others], he seemed to be in quest of mental food, not heart sustenance" (p. 178). But the relation between the two men is much closer. For one thing, we know that Clifford is "really" a Maule. For another, we learn that the younger man's nature somehow requires that he observe, "feed off of" we should say, the old man's sufferings:

> Holgrave took some pains to establish an intercourse with Clifford, actuated, it might seem, entirely by an impulse of kindliness. . . . Nevertheless, in the artist's deep, thoughtful, all-observant eyes, there was, now and then, an expression not sinister, but questionable; as if he had some other interest in the scene than a stranger, a youthful and unconnected adventurer, might be supposed to have. [P. 156]

Later, we are told that "always, in his interviews with Phoebe, the artist made especial inquiry as to the welfare of Clifford" (p. 178). Still later, Holgrave appears as a kind of double for Hawthorne, when Phoebe criticizes him for a criminally omniscient relationship to her aunt and uncle: "You talk as if this old house were a theater . . . you seem to look at [their] misfortunes . . . as a tragedy . . . played exclusively for your amusement" (p. 217).

Only Hawthorne could be so perversely self-reductive. Phoebe's criticism twists the aesthetic relation of author to the creatures of his brain into a moral condemnation of detachment. Phoebe can be said to criticize Holgrave for depersonalizing the tragic lives of Clifford and Hepzibah, for relating to them as the imago-projecting schizophrenic relates to real people. Yet the subtile process endorses Holgrave's preoccupation with Clifford, for the two are related, I would argue, as developmental phases of selfhood. Clifford is an adolescent self, the passing of which releases, by means of Hawthorne's "spiritualized machinery" of plot structure, the mature self. "Our first youth is of no value," says Holgrave. "But sometimes . . . there comes a sense of second youth, gushing out of the heart's joy at being in love" (p. 215).

This is how the machinery works: during the train episode, Clifford *becomes* Holgrave, while Holgrave, paralyzed by Jaffrey, *becomes* Clifford. The movement is worked out temporally from a hellish timelessness (Clifford's condition at the beginning), to time unhealthily transcended (Clifford on the train), to time caught up with (Holgrave and Phoebe marry and are assimilated by society). The man who was simultaneously infantile and senescent becomes, finally, the man who is simply his proper age. Very much a part of the man's coming-to-be is his ceasing to be an artist. Let us look at how Hawthorne concludes his romance, not only to prove a theory, but also to see firsthand the romancer practicing an art that claims to take liberties with novelistic conventions of time and identity "without swerv[ing] aside from the truth of the human heart" (p. 1).

First: Clifford becomes Holgrave. In an earlier chapter, "it seemed to Holgrave . . . that in this age . . . the moss-grown and rotten Past is to be torn down, and lifeless institutions to be thrust out of the way, and their corpses buried, and everything to begin anew" (p. 179). Later he exclaims:

> "Shall we never, never get rid of this Past? . . . It lies upon the Present like a giant's dead body! In fact, the case is just as if a young giant were compelled to waste all his strength in carrying about the corpse of the old giant, his grandfather, who died a long while ago, and only needs to be decently buried. Just think a moment, and it will startle you to see what slaves we are to bygone times—to Death, if we give the matter the right word!" [Pp. 182–83]

Finally, he expresses the trust that "we shall live to see the day . . . when no man shall build his house for posterity. . . . It were better that they should crumble to ruin once in twenty years" (pp. 183–84), to which Phoebe replies, "it makes me dizzy to think of such a shifting world."

Clifford on the train realizes this mental condition of dizziness, Hawthorne's negative version of afflatus, and ascends to a world "set adrift" and "unfixed" (p. 256), the "pathless" (p. 306), *Extravagant* world Phoebe fears. The words he speaks during his "flight," both a literal running away and a "flight of ideas," are pure Holgrave:

> "My impression is that our wonderfully increased and still increas-

ing facilities of locomotion are destined to bring us round again to the nomadic state." [P. 259] ". . . the greatest possible stumbling blocks in the path of human happiness and improvement are these heaps of bricks and stones, consolidated with mortar, . . . which men painfully contrive for their own torment, and call them house and home!" [P. 201]

"A man will commit almost any wrong—he will heap up an immense pile of wickedness, as hard as granite, and which will weigh as heavily upon his soul to eternal ages—only to build a great, gloomy, dark-chambered mansion, for himself to die in, and for his posterity to be miserable in. He lays his own dead corpse beneath the underpinning . . . and, after converting himself into an evil destiny, expects his remotest great-grandchildren to be happy there!" [P. 263]

Meanwhile, Holgrave becomes Clifford, literally petrified by the anxiety provoked by the presence of the dead Jaffrey. The corpse casts a pall of guilt on his life, as the living Jaffrey had cast over Clifford's, deprives him of future possibility, as Jaffrey had stolen Clifford's future, and takes away his youth, as Jaffrey's frame-up of Clifford had caused the latter's youth to be spent in prison. Holgrave says:

"In all our lives there can never come another moment like that! . . . Phoebe, is it all terror—nothing but terror. . . . The presence of yonder dead threw a great black shadow over everything; he made the universe . . . a scene of guilt and retribution more dreadful than the guilt. The sense of it took away my youth. I never hoped to feel young again. The world looked strange, wild, evil, hostile; my past life, so lonesome and dreary; my future a shapeless gloom, which I must mold into gloomy shapes!" [Pp. 305–6]

Holgrave's existence, in short, has become, like Clifford's, *Extravagant*. He has wandered too far and is, as he says, "all astray" (p. 302), suffering from "matters that fall far out of the ordinary rule" (p. 301), and is desperate "to betake himself within the precincts of common life" (p. 305). But the stalled mountain climber needs outside help "to bring him back into the breathing world . . . the common track of things" (p. 140). The crowning similarity between the old man and the young man is that both are rescued from their dreaded "being-beyond-the-world" by Phoebe. "You are my only possibility of happiness!", Holgrave tells her. Life became a living hell, "but, Phoebe, you crossed the threshold. . . . The black moment at once became a blissful one" (p. 306). Holgrave's "black moment" is a condensation of Clifford's whole life. The simplest

way of explaining the connection of the two men is to quote the
tale upon which *The Seven Gables* was based, "Peter
Goldthwaite's Treasure" (1838). Although the hero of that tale
is seventy years old, "the true, the essential Peter was a young
man of high hopes, just entering on the world" (9:392). Clifford is Peter, and the true, essential, young Clifford is reified as
a character in his own right, Holgrave.

IV

In a letter to Horatio Bridge, Hawthorne called *The Seven
Gables* a work "more characteristic of my mind, and more
proper and natural for me to write, than 'The Scarlet Letter';
but for that very reason, less likely to interest the public."[13] It is
more characteristic of his mind, one could say, because its
proper subject is the characteristics of that mind viewed in a
typically negative light. While it is to Hawthorne's credit to have
been able to include as a level of meaning within his work the
kind of reading a clinically minded critic of this century would
exhume, it is nevertheless paradoxical that an artist should en-
tertain a theory of his art so inimical to its practitioner and so
discouraging to further practicing it. For Hawthorne, an imag-
ined world is not an ultimate elegance, but a disease. *The Seven
Gables* is thus autobiographical in a way that transcends the
historical details the author borrowed from his family's Puritan
past. It is autobiographical less in the sense of strict borrowings
from a man's actual life than in the sense of the life history of
an imagination, of an author looking over his past creations in
order to find some sequence of intelligible development. This
issue, although it is beyond the scope of the present essay, is
something Hawthorne wants us—or at least the reader who is
sufficiently attuned to the machinations of his "nonsense"—to
realize. The point is made with his characteristically cute bizarreness in the figure of a little boy named Ned Higgins, whose
initials are the same as the author's own. Like Clifford and
Holgrave, little Ned is very oral; indeed, he does nothing in the
entire book but eat every time he appears. This "little cannibal"
(p. 50), Hawthorne's secret "signature," eats only gingerbread,
but like Laing's schizophrenic, who wishes to incorporate all of
reality and turn it to dust and ashes, Ned is allowed to ingest all
of creation, albeit in cookie form. Of Ned it is said:

This remarkable urchin, in truth, was the very emblem of old

Father Time, both in respect of his all-devouring appetite for men and things, and because he, as well as Time, after engulfing this much of creation, looked almost as youthful as if he had been just that moment made. [P. 115]

Nor is Ned without his share of violence, and the author describes his appearance in Hepzibah's shop as wreaking "an irreparable ruin . . . as if his childish gripe had torn down the seven-gabled mansion" (p. 51).

Hawthorne's nonsense here, I would suggest, has apocalyptic implications. It is said of Owen Warland, "The Artist of the Beautiful," who, like Hawthorne in *The Seven Gables,* is an artist in the medium of subjectivized time, that "he would turn the sun out of its orbit and derange the whole course of time, if his ingenuity could grasp anything larger than a child's toy" (RE, 2:505). If Owen is a maker of apocalyptic children's toys, Ned Higgins is Hawthorne's portrait of the apocalyptic Romantic artist as a child. We are used to the idea of Romantic apocalypse from Shelley (Hawthorne's favorite poet) and Blake, but even in a book as concerned with tearing down the old as *The Seven Gables* is, the application of the notion to Hawthorne may seem absurd; indeed, Hawthorne *makes* it absurd. Nevertheless, Clifford on the train transcends both space and time, speeding up the second to an unbearable pitch, while Hawthorne brings time to a halt by having the dead Jaffrey's watch wind down and stop. Notice also that at the outset of Clifford's flight, the author writes, "they were wandering all abroad, on . . . a pilgrimage . . . *to the world's end*" (p. 253; italics mine). This apocalyptic statement is qualified, however—and typically—as "precisely such a pilgrimage *as a child often meditates.*"

The House of the Seven Gables finally retreats from such implications, but it is a book in which a last judgment does occur, a last judgment that the author passes upon himself. It is the story of his own withdrawn and long-drawn-out youth, his own schizophrenia, or better, his own despair, or possibly best of all, his own "upward fall" into *Extravagance,* a disease which "artists are particularly susceptible to" and "which, rather than hysteria or melancholy, appears as the pathological aspect of the poetic personality."[14] In the romance Hawthorne is able to conceive of an alternative to the artist's *Extravagance,* a way down and back, but part of the return trip requires relinquishing the identity of an artist:

Why are poets so apt to choose their mates not for any similarity of poetic endowment, but for qualities which might make the happiness of the rudest handicraftsman as well as that of the ideal craftsman of the spirit? Because, probably, at his highest elevation, the poet needs no human intercourse; but he finds it dreary to descend, and be a stranger. [P. 141]

For Hawthorne, unlike Blake, the "Real Man" is not "the Imagination." Indeed, to become real at all—and becoming real is conceived as a breath-taking acquisition in *The Seven Gables*—means sloughing off the Clifford part of the personality, not in favor of a newly defined, non-*Extravagant* artist, but in favor of just being a "real" man. In Hawthorne's version, art is a stage—and a potentially deadly one—one passes through before becoming an authentic person.

1. Nathaniel Hawthorne, *The House of the Seven Gables, Centenary Edition of the Works of Nathaniel Hawthorne* (Columbus, Ohio: Ohio State University Press, 1965), 2:26. All further quotations from the romance are from volume 2 and page numbers are cited in parentheses in the text. Wherever possible, quotations from other of Hawthorne's works refer to this Centenary Edition; volume and page numbers are cited in the text. Where the Centenary Edition has not yet published a work, the so-called Riverside Edition (Boston: Houghton, Mifflin and Company, 1882), indicated as RE, is used.

2. Frederick Crews, *The Sins of the Fathers* (New York: Oxford University Press, 1966).

3. The "peculiar excellence [of Priscilla's purses], besides the great delicacy and beauty of the manufacture, lay in the almost impossibility that any uninitiated person should discover the aperture; although, to a practiced touch, they would open as wide as charity or prodigality." The repressed narrator then "wonder[s] if it were not a symbol of Priscilla's own mystery" (3:35).

4. That the hidden meaning of the passage is ludicrous and seemingly nonsensical should enhance the feeling that Hawthorne is intentionally, and with a characteristic playfulness not often noticed, up to some "baby play" (p. 149). I say this because nonsense is a recurrent word in his vocabulary, and it is regularly applied when literature is the issue at hand. Speaking of himself as "M. de l'Aubépine" in the prefatory note to "Rappaccini's Daughter," he avers that his "productions, if the reader chance to take them in precisely the proper point of view, may amuse a leisure hour as well as those of a brighter man; if otherwise, they can hardly fail to look excessively like nonsense" (RE 2:108). Miles Coverdale, the narrator of *The Blithedale Romance*, has the following conversation with another character on the subject of poetic influence:

"You seem," said Hollingsworth, "to be trying how much nonsense you can pour out in a breath."

"I wish you would see fit to comprehend," retorted [Coverdale], "that the profoundest wisdom must be mingled with nine-tenths of nonsense, else it is not worth the breath that utters it." [3:129]

A twice-told tale—the Hawthornian mode par excellence—spoken by Zenobia in the same romance is prefaced by the following words: "From beginning to end, it was undeniable nonsense, but not necessarily the worse for that" (3:108).

5. Austin Warren, *Rage for Order* (Ann Arbor, Mich.: University of Michigan Press, 1948), p. 99.

6. R. D. Laing, *The Divided Self* (Baltimore, Md.: Penguin Books, 1965), p. 39. Further references from this book will be cited in parentheses in the text as L, followed by page numbers.

7. Jay Leyda, ed., *The Portable Melville* (New York: Viking Press, 1952), p. 406.

8. See Ludwig Binswanger, "Extravagance," in *Being-in-the-World* (New York: Harper & Row, 1967), pp. 342–49.

9. Ironically, Hawthorne later refers to Clifford's behavior at the arched window as "extravagances," and Jaffrey, who employs the term, is threatening to have Clifford committed. It is no coincidence, since the author is clearly playing upon the etymology of *extravagant*, wandering beyond the conditions of actuality.

10. Soren Kierkegaard, *The Sickness unto Death*, trans. Walter Lowrie (Garden City, N.Y.: Doubleday, 1954), p. 164.

11. Binswanger, "Extravagance," p. 347.

12. The following passage from *The Scarlet Letter* is Hawthorne's most concise, "realistic" description of the dangers of the *vol imaginaire*. Notice how Hester becomes *Extravagant*, getting lost on a "precipice" in her reverie, how the world loses materiality, becoming a nightmare, and how she cannot come back from this visionary cul-de-sac to the ordinary track of things except by committing suicide or murder:

the same question often rose into her mind, with reference to the whole race of womanhood. Was existence worth accepting, even to the happiest among them? As concerned her own individual existence, she had long ago decided in the negative, and dismissed the point as settled. A tendency to speculation, though it may keep woman quiet, as it does man, yet makes her sad. She discerns, it may be, such a hopeless task before her. As a first step, the whole system of society is to be torn down, and built up anew. Then, the very nature of the opposite sex, or its long hereditary habit, which has become like nature, is to be essentially modified, before woman can be allowed to assume what seems a fair and suitable position. Finally, all other difficulties being obviated, woman cannot take advantage of these preliminary reforms, until she herself shall have undergone a still mightier change: in which, perhaps, the ethereal essence, wherein she has her truest life, will be found to have evaporated. A woman never overcomes these problems by any exercise of thought. They are not to be solved, or only in one way. If her heart chance to come uppermost, they vanish. Thus, Hester Prynne, whose heart had lost its regular and healthy throb, wandered without a clew in the dark labyrinth of mind; now turned aside by an unsurmountable precipice; now starting back from a deep chasm. There was wild and ghastly scenery all around her and a home and comfort nowhere. At times, a fearful doubt strove to possess her soul, whether it were not better to send Pearl at once to heaven, and go herself to such futurity as Eternal Justice should provide. [1:165–66]

13. Horatio Bridge, *Personal Recollections of Nathaniel Hawthorne* (New York: Harper & Brothers, 1893), p. 126.

14. Paul de Man, *Blindness and Insight* (New York: Oxford University Press, 1971), pp. 46, 47.

Style, Science, Technology, and William Carlos Williams

Lisa M. Steinman

Reed College

I

WILLIAM CARLOS WILLIAMS's writings, like the writings of many of his contemporaries, show a concern about the place and function of poetry in the modern world. As he asks in his 1914 "The Wanderer," the poem with which he chooses to open his *Collected Earlier Poems:* "How shall I be a mirror to this modernity?" (*CEP*, p. 3).[1] Williams's connections to other modern artists and writers have been well documented; and recent criticism has begun to notice his use of Einstein and the Curies in his later poetry.[2] My purpose here is to explore the role that popular debates, and misconceptions, about science and technology play in Williams's development of a definition of literary modernism.

Williams admits to having been unclear about what, exactly, influenced his early modernist experiments, saying: "What were we seeking? No one knew consistently enough to formulate a 'movement.' We were . . . closely allied with the painters. . . . We had followed Pound's instructions" (*A*, p. 148). As Williams confesses here, his early poetry seems sometimes to rest its case for being "a mirror to . . . modernity" simply on its association with other, well-publicized, avant-garde movements. Williams's early theoretical writings also bear witness to his confusion about the nature of modernity and its relationship to modernism. Since the modernist redefinition of the arts involved the rethinking of the nature and purpose of the arts, however, the question of poetry's role in modern society needed to be addressed, as did the related question of how modernity should be defined.

For Williams, as for others in America in the first decades of this century, modernity and progress seem linked, at least in part, to advances in what was popularly called "science." As Leo Stein explains in his 1917 article "American Optimism," "machinery and innumerable substances of value to industry became rapidly available, and . . . the advance in the mastery and control of material conditions became orderly and continuous" (*The Seven Arts*, May 1917, p. 79). Stein goes on to say that the confidence bred by technological discoveries is a false confidence in that it ignores the problem of which values will inform the direction taken by technology, and he proposes science as a source of the reforms he finds necessary. The article finally calls for a "social *science*" (p. 84; emphasis added), which is to be founded by men comparable to Lister or Pasteur (p. 82) and to revitalize science and the arts alike by providing a "soul's hygiene" (p. 84). While Stein begins by distinguishing between the scientist and the engineer, his final analogy between the hygiene already provided by science and a spiritual hygiene needed by society blurs the distinction between science and technology.

It is illuminating to juxtapose Stein's optimistic view of science and technology with another view, which received some publicity at the same time. Just as Stein's article appeared, Duchamp resigned from the organizing committee for the Independents Exhibition in New York. Despite their announced policy of deploring censorship, the committee refused to accept the porcelain urinal which he anonymously submitted to the show. In the May 1917 issue of *The Blind Man*, Duchamp pronounces judgment on American taste: "The only works of art America has given are her plumbing and her bridges" (no. 2 [May 1917], p. 5). Duchamp's admiration for the look of American plumbing and bridges is genuine; however, his remarks are intended to shock his audience. Those who refused to accept his urinal could hardly have been expected to agree with his judgment on American plumbing; celebrations of American technology and hygiene, such as Stein's, did not view technological products as artistic per se. As Duchamp's problem with the Independents suggests, it was not clear how art might participate in the modernity for which hygiene stood.

I have juxtaposed Stein's and Duchamp's articles as emblematic of two radically different ways in which American technology and science (popularly confused with each other) were viewed. On the one hand, technological progress and hygiene seem emblematic of a system of values—including materialism, efficiency, and perhaps Puritan squeamishness—unlikely to provide an environment in which the arts might flourish. On the other hand, technology seems to be the distinguishing positive feature of the modernity which the arts wished to capture and to which they wished to lay claim.

Any reader of *The Blind Man* and *The Seven Arts* in May of 1917 might have been struck by these ironically juxtaposed concepts of American hygiene. Williams read both journals and echoes Duchamp, whom he admired, in his later references to "American plumbing [and] . . . American bridges" (*SE*, p. 35).[3] It is pleasing to imagine that the shock of reading Duchamp and Stein together is responsible for Williams's further, repeated, sarcasm about the hygienic inventions of modern America, its "bathrooms, kitchens, [and] hospitals" (*IAG*, p. 177) or "modern plumbing [and] refrigeration" (*SE*, p. 176). However, Williams's use of such images may not be a matter of direct influence, but simply another acknowledgment of the widespread fascination with technology.

The juxtaposition of Stein, Duchamp, and Williams shows that the relationship between modernity (in the form of technology) and literary or artistic modernism was complicated. The relationship is further complicated by the fact that many artists looking for a modern style took as a model "the accuracy, the fine finish, and the unerring fidelity to design" found in the products of modern technology, a point made implicitly by Duchamp and explicitly by writers such as Lewis Mumford, whose article "Machinery and the Modern Style" (*The New Republic*, 3 August 1921, p. 264) contains the above description of an accurate, finely finished, tightly designed style.[4] As Mumford proposes in *American Taste*, "the celebration of the more austere forms of science and mechanics" may have been "the major intellectual impulse in back of Cubism."[5] In any case, many modernists, both in art and in poetry, were intrigued by what might be called a machine aesthetic.

Artists may not need to think deeply about the practical, historical relationship between their art and the rise of technology in order to borrow a style from technology. Yet modernism did claim to redefine the role of the arts in a world which it obviously saw to be characterized by the rise of technology. Moreover, the modernist poets who borrowed their style from technology were, typically, self-conscious about style. Stevens, for instance, suggests that aesthetic ideas might be "tantamount to moral ideas,"[6] while Williams proclaims style, albeit "ghost-like," to be "the substance of writing" (*SE*, p. 75). Thus, at least in theory, style is of fundamental importance, and the adoption of a poetic style related to technology raises the difficult question of poetry's relationship to a technological society. Williams, in particular, found it necessary to raise and try to answer this question.

II

From the early volumes of poetry, *Sour Grapes* and *Spring and All,* through the 1934 volume of *Collected Poems,* published by The Objectivist Press, and the 1935 *An Early Martyr,* Williams experiments with what I have called a machine aesthetic. Indeed, he is probably best known for the sparse, hard-edged use of language found in early poems such as "The Red Wheelbarrow," "The Locust Tree in Flower," or "Young Sycamore."[7] Further, the question of such poetry's role in modern society was particularly pressing for Williams because of his decision not to follow Pound and others to Europe. Williams thus found himself needing to defend his allegiance to a culture which, from one point of view, could not understand, let alone foster, pieces such as Duchamp's urinal. Specifically, Williams seems to have felt the need to show that his life as a doctor in America, and his daily contact with people who were neither literary nor avant-garde, provided the best possible setting in which to develop a new poetry. At the same time, many of the same aspects of popular American culture which Williams defends—its attention to practical matters and its sometimes naive optimism, which Stein's article relates to practical, technological progress in America—seem partial causes for the alienation of just those expatriates to whom Williams addresses his defense.[8]

It is clear that Williams's defense of America as the birthplace of modernism rests on his awareness that America is distinctively modern because of its technology and industrial "know-how." In 1922, for instance, we find him engaged in defending practical American ingenuity as that which should inform American poetry:

Not that Americans today can be anything less than citizens of the world; but being inclined to run off to London and Paris it is

inexplicable that in every case they have forgotten or not known
that the experience of native local contacts, which they take with
them, is the only thing that can give that differentiated quality of
presentation to their work which at first enriches their new sphere
and later alone might carry them far as creative artists in the continental hurly-burly. Pound ran off to Europe in a hurry. It is under-
standable. But he had not sufficient ground to stand on for more
than perhaps two years. . . . It has been by paying naked attention
first to the thing itself that American plumbing . . . indexing systems, locomotives, printing presses, city buildings, farm imple-
ments and a thousand other things have become notable in the
world. Yet we are timid in believing that in the arts discovery and
invention will take the same course. And there is no reason why
they should unless our writers have the inventive intelligence of
our engineers and cobblers. [*SE*, p. 35][9]

Williams desires to defend American modernism by appealing
to America's prowess in engineering. Leaving aside for the moment the identification of the engineer's strength as inventive
intelligence, or creativity, it is clear that the *fame* of American
plumbing and indexing systems involves both commercial success and tangible results. For poems to echo, indeed, to borrow
some of their authority from, achievements in other fields
where results are more tangible and more lucrative presents a
problem: how are poets to follow engineers? When Stein calls
for a social science or Frank A. Manny, whose article also appears in *The Seven Arts,* concludes that art "like industry must
achieve visible and tangible results which minister to human
use" (June 1917, p. 223), their language takes the hard results
of technology as the measure of advances in the arts. Yet if
poetry, like plumbing, is to be justified by its tangible results,
how can it be justified at all?

Despite this problem, Williams frequently allies himself with
the practical American vision represented by Stein and Manny.
In his *Autobiography,* for instance, looking back on his trip
abroad, he has a young French salesman admit that the French
"methods are not as quick or efficient as yours" (*A*, p. 192).
However, in his defense of American efficiency and practi-
cality, Williams betrays some insecurity. In the same chapter of
the *Autobiography,* he presents himself as a practical, unsophis-
ticated American in his confrontation with Ford Madox Ford,
one of the giants of European modernism: "What had I to say
with all eyes, especially those of the Frenchmen, gimleted upon
me to see what this American could possibly signify, if any-

thing? I had nothing in common with them. I . . . sat down feeling like a fool" (A, p. 195).

While Williams's pose as an outsider, a fool, is partly ironic, the irony is uneasy. If practical America held the key to the modern world, Ford and others seemed to be right that practical America, which measured success by utility, had no use for modern poetry. Williams registers this fact, if not always clearly. His poem "Pastoral" displays the hard-edged, clean, and accurate modern style associated with American technology.[10] The poem appears in the same year as Stein's and Manny's articles comparing poetry and technology, and ends after having described the beauty of a poor neighborhood: "No one / will believe this / of vast import to the nation" (CEP, p. 121). The America Williams claims as his own is in fact interested in quite another kind of import (and export), with which poetry, practically speaking, cannot compete.

Williams does, however, propose another view of what technology reveals about the American character, which tries to avoid the comparison between the tangible or profitable results of technology and the results of poetry. His suggestion that poets "take the same course" as engineers documents the success of American engineers by producing a long list of successful inventions, but he also celebrates inventive intelligence, or the imaginative energy of American inventors, evidenced by such goods. Williams is not alone in finding a creative spirit behind the often dismal results of industrial growth. The Seven Arts, which printed both Stein's and Manny's articles, also presented Russell's declaration that one can see "fundamental [i.e., creative] work" in science, and Oppenheim's description of the "glow of the human spirit in the laboratory" (October 1917, p. 682 and June 1917, p. 229).[11]

This reevaluation of technology, and by association science, is important: technological society may appear at first glance to have no use for poetry, but on closer inspection, technological progress is seen to require the creativity which is most clearly the province of the arts. More importantly, by not being tied to commerce—precisely by not producing results like factories and plastics—poetry offers what is essentially valuable in modern technology in, as it were, a purer form.

In his dialogue concerning the relationship between architecture and poetry, Williams says that "in a scientific era . . . the artist's protest that his art is wholly nonutilitarian has a certain

amount of truth in it. . . . The uselessness of it might constitute
its principal use, sometimes" (SE, p. 179).[12] His point is that art
is important, but its usefulness cannot be taken as analogous to
the uses of electricity, "modern plumbing, refrigeration,
autos," or, as Williams adds sarcastically, "twin beds" (SE,
p. 176). Especially in architecture, modernity might seem to
consist of these external trappings, but the essay suggests that
the breakdown of the analogy between the uses of art and the
uses of technology shows the value of art which does not separate people (in twin beds) or lead to a lack of the contact which
Williams defines as a distinctly American virtue. The argument,
then, is that art, while possessing many of the virtues of science,
is not implicated in the production of things such as "bathrooms, kitchens, [and] hospitals," which are denounced as bars
"to more intimate shocks" (IAG, p. 177), as ways of avoiding
contact. In short, the uselessness of art becomes its strength.

  Williams uses his new analogy between scientific and artistic
creativity to place poetry on firmer ground. Thus, his late version of Pasteur, unlike Stein's prototype of a social scientist, is a
man interested in "theory" (SSA, p. 62), not results, and the
1918 "Prologue" to Kora in Hell denounces "a science doing
slavey service upon gas engines" in favor of "inventive imagination" and "the authentic spirit of change" (I, p. 13) which do not
rest content with any particular invention. Having reassessed
the strengths of science, Williams can insist upon the superiority of poetry. Again, in The Embodiment of Knowledge, he compares Shakespeare and Bacon: both men are creative, but
Shakespeare is used to dramatize the fact that creativity is more
important than its results. As another of Williams's essays explains, Shakespeare makes "objects, realities which he has to
abandon to make another, and another—perfectly blank to him
as soon as they are completed" (SE, p. 56). In The Embodiment of
Knowledge, Williams discusses machinery (meaning literal machines, poems, and knowledge in general)[13] in similar terms:
"As soon as we make it we must at once plan to escape—and
escape" (EK, p. 62), adding that the problem with the engineer
is that his knowledge "being so in particular, is likely to absorb
him into itself until he becomes a scientist [here, obviously, a
technocrat]—limited, segregated—unable to escape" (EK,
p. 63). It is not surprising, then, that the next section of The
Embodiment of Knowledge compares Bacon, unfavorably, to
Shakespeare.

  Williams's analysis of how poetry and science have a common

ground is appealing. Yet in order to defend the value of poets in light of their practical historical situation, it is not sufficient to note the inventive intelligence which informs scientific work as well as the arts, or even to propose, as Williams does in the examples offered above, that the arts escape the taint of technology. Indeed, the *success* of science and technology does not seem to rest most immediately upon the pure imagination of scientists, but upon tangible and commercially successful products. If this is true, Williams's position presents problems, since it is precisely this practical success which he wants to appropriate for poetry, even while he casts doubt on science and technology because of their ties to commercialism.

The desire to claim for poetry the popular and commercial success enjoyed by science is not limited to Williams: one need only think of I. A. Richards's (1924) project in *Principles of Literary Criticism* and of R. S. Crane's objections to Richards's scientism.[14] However, Williams's double endeavor—to defend modern poetry and to define a distinctly American modern poetry in terms of the modern American experience—helps clarify the tensions involved in this common strategy for the defense of poetry.

The tensions are obvious in Williams's censure (quoted above) of scientific knowledge as being too "in particular," a phrase uncomfortably close to the attention to particulars and to things in themselves he wants to celebrate in American poetry and to ground in the success of American technology. Not surprisingly, Williams's confusion (about how to defend against the threat posed by technology a style borrowed from and justified by technology) is most clearly dramatized in the portions of his early books where he justifies his position as a modernist in modern America.

In *In the American Grain,* Williams pronounces that the actual schemes, like the actual products, of scientists, saints, and philosophers "amount to nothing. But to the men themselves every moment, every detail, the devotion, the clarities are vital—and so we value them, in short, by their style" (*IAG,* p. 207). We find a familiar shift here: scientists, saints, and philosophers (like the inventors of American technological products) are important not only because of their creativity, but because of a certain style of operation, including a detailed attention to particulars. Thus, it is a style, not the results of a style, which is important. Of course, Williams's description of the style of creative men is, in part, a description of the style of technological products or inventions, as well as of a scientific method of proceeding. Here, however, he dismisses specific creations to concentrate on the process of creating. At the same time, he debunks the detailed, focused method of proceeding, that is, the scientific method, when practiced by men of science rather than by poets. Franklin's "itch to serve science" and "to do the little concrete thing" (*IAG*, p. 155) is found lacking, as is the scientist's urge to keep things "cold and small and under the cold lens" (*IAG*, p. 175). Williams's claim seems to be that by paying too much attention to the practical results of their work, scientists deny the creative force of their own methods. Yet the aura of importance surrounding science, precisely because of its practical results, is something Williams claims for *himself* in his late self-description as one trained with "the humility and caution of the scientist" (*A*, p. 58). At the same time, the inventor Franklin is censoriously described as "the full development of the timidity, the strength that denies itself" (*IAG*, p. 155). Similarly, Williams's style in *The Great American Novel*—a grab bag of anecdotes and images—is distinguished from the quilt made of rags mechanically encased in silkolene, an image of loss of contact which ends the novel.

Such attempts to appropriate certain features of science and technology for poets, while denying these features to scientists, are, if not convincing, nonetheless revelatory of the tensions in the larger social and historical contexts I have just outlined. I have suggested some reasons why Williams, especially, illuminates the challenge science and technology seem to have posed the American writer. Having sketched the broader context in which Williams's writings appear, I should like to offer a reading, in accordance with Williams's stated poetics, of one of the poems in which he relies on the modern style which I have related to a machine aesthetic, and then to comment further upon how Williams's poetry dramatizes the tensions implicit in his strategy of appropriating the success of science and technology for poetry.

III

The poem I have chosen is characteristically brief:

Young Sycamore

I must tell you
this young tree

> whose round and firm trunk
> between the wet
>
> pavement and the gutter
> (where water
> is trickling) rises
> bodily
>
> into the air with
> one undulant
> thrust half its height—
> and then
>
> dividing and waning
> sending out
> young branches on
> all sides—
>
> hung with cocoons
> it thins
> till nothing is left of it
> but two
>
> eccentric knotted
> twigs
> bending forward
> hornlike at the top
>
> [CEP, p. 332]

Poems such as "Young Sycamore" seem to resist explication, to be purely descriptive, although—as J. Hillis Miller points out—Williams takes a firm stance against "the falseness of attempting to 'copy' nature" (I, p. 107), desiring "not 'realism' but reality itself" (I, p. 117). Miller's argument that the poem does not represent a tree but rather "is an object which has the same kind of life as the tree," sounds convincing.[15] If, as he argues, "Young Sycamore" is not symbolic but an object in its own right, it nonetheless presents an analogy between the growth of a tree and the growth of a poem: the motion described is paradigmatic, familiar to any reader of Kora in Hell, Spring and All, or In the American Grain.[16] The tree's "bodily" rise ending in the near still life of the two twigs is a motion very like Williams's description of imaginative creation.[17] In 1936, for instance, in "How to Write," Williams says that poems begin with "the very muscles and bones of the body itself speaking," although "once the writing is on paper it becomes an object. . . . an object for the liveliest attention that the full mind can give it" (SSA, p. 98). Thus, we have a series of parallel motions: nature produces the tree (in a fashion very close to the way we have seen the produc-

tion of inventions described); Williams produces his poem; and
the reader is invited to join in the creative process, not by looking through language to that which it describes, but by paying
attention to the poem itself, and, if the paradigm of the poet
and nature holds, producing some object of his own.

Even without knowing Williams's theories about poetry,
when we turn our full minds and attention to the poem-as-
object, we find ourselves referred to Williams's process of creation in language. It seems no accident that the verbs, like the
tree, thin out toward the end of the poem, nor that the one
simile occurs in the last line, as the flow of language ends. In
view of Williams's usual avoidance of similes,[18] the overt figure
at the end of "Young Sycamore" calls attention to the language
of the poem. It shifts our attention from trees to poems, and
recasts the poem as an emblem or, at least, as a series of figures:
not only is the tree's growth like the poet's creative process, but
the waxing and waning of the tree is echoed more succinctly in
the cocoons' simultaneous image of death and potential life—
contradictory motions finally abstracted in the stark duality of
the two twigs.[19]

The central concern of the poem seems to be the process of
growth or creation with its inevitable culmination in a product.
But products can yield new realities, new life, like the cocoons
or the emblem of the eccentric twigs. The twigs are eccentric
because the literal center of the poem images the process of
creation yielding both multiplicity and destruction as the
trunk's "one undulant / thrust" begins to divide and wane between the third and fourth stanzas. The final image is eccentric
as well because the twigs, while tempting us to align their duality with the other dualities to which the poem calls our attention—the process behind the product; the destruction in creation (and vice versa); the poem as object and figure, physical
and intellectual—remain stubbornly particular. As Williams
says, delaying the noun by a stanza break and line of adjectives
so that "two" seems for a moment the object itself, "nothing is
left of it / but two." The final duality is purely formal or structural.

One might say that all of the oppositions suggested in the
poem are given their purest expression—not resolved, but expressed—in the image which is the fruition of the poem, but
which is so well "knotted" that nothing remains to be said: "the
detail is its own solution." In fact, the hornlike twigs encapsu-
late the dilemma posed by this poem, which both is and is about

a unique object even as it suggests that all objects, once subjected to lively attention, can be made (in the thrill of discovery) to release a creative energy which necessarily transcends the discrete structure of individual objects. At the same time, the result of this creative energy seems to be the revelation of a structure, and there is even some indication that, as the life of the poem is parallel to the life of the tree, creativity is itself another version of the formal structure imaged by the entire movement of the poem—from the poet's presence, insisted upon in the first line (which roots the poem in a creative, human, speaker), to the final image which repeats the formal essence of the poem and the tree.

Williams often images the force or energy of poems as an "essence" or "rare presence" (A, p. 362). These images occur quite early in his writing: a 1921 editorial in Contact, discussing Burke's article on Laforgue, describes the search for a "milligram of radium" (SE, p. 36), while the essay on Marianne Moore published in A Novelette and Other Prose speaks of the "white light that is the background of all good work" (SE, p. 122). In the Rasles section of In the American Grain, Williams isolates a "core of nature" (IAG, p. 105) within himself, analogous to "the strange phosphorus of the life" (IAG, p. v) sought throughout the book, all images of an incandescent universal presence which is in back of or perhaps in all art and all natural objects. I will refer to the scientific sources of these images later, but for now I would like to question the status of this "essence." In "Young Sycamore," at least, it is presented as a structure. A reading of the poem's "essence" as purely formal and finally impersonal is reinforced by the poem's use of language: the sparse, unembellished lines and vocabulary, like the imagistic progression of the poem, add to this effect.

To see poems as impersonal is, of course, a commonplace of modernist poetics, and the link between this view of poetry and science is widely noted. Eliot, for instance, to pick a poet with whom Williams generally takes issue, suggests that it is in "depersonalization that art may be said to approach the condition of science."[20] Williams's description of the use of language in poems such as "Young Sycamore" similarly invokes science, as when he approvingly says in his 1931 review of Marianne Moore's poetry that words are "separated out by science, treated with acid to remove the smudges, washed, dried and placed right side up on a clean surface" (SE, p. 128).

It is worth noting, again, Williams's conflation of science and laboratory technology as well as his use of yet another image of science as hygiene. More important, however, is Williams's recognition that his insistence upon objects and their formal structures, central to the style and content of "Young Sycamore," is linked to technology. The link, indeed, is subtle: the poem not only appeals to a taste for clean lines and efficiency fostered by industrial technology, but is defined as a discrete structure, a "machine made of words" which does not need to refer outside of itself for its effect since its "movement is intrinsic" (*SE,* p. 256), as Williams says. One can, indeed, go further in detailing the ways in which Williams's mixed response to technology informs his view of poetry.

Williams justifies the machine aesthetic of poems like "Young Sycamore" by citing the need to reclaim the essence of poems, trees, and other objects "nameless under an old misappellation" (*IAG,* p. v) with a new, cleaner language to be provided by the poet. What the poet reclaims, then, in "Young Sycamore" for instance, is not a particular tree, but a method of reclamation, and, as we have seen, an essential structure which is purely formal. In fact, the reference in "Young Sycamore" to the poet's process of creation recasts the cycle of creation and destruction itself not only within but as a formal structure.

Forcing Williams's poetics to one possible conclusion: it is not that poems, more self-consciously than machines, reveal human inventiveness, but that knowledge, language, poems, plants, and men are structurally similar, and their structural essence is best described by analogy to machines or technological products.[21] The human imagination itself is thus reenvisioned as a mechanism which is presented in the formal structure of the poem largely by analogy.

Williams's humanism generally prevents him from fully embracing this view to which his acceptance of a certain style seems, at times, to commit him. In his 1937 dialogue on poetry and architecture, for example, he tries to explain why he rejects, as he says, the "'back to humanity, back to the soil' business" about the organic production of art, while still believing that people are "the origin of every bit of life that can possibly inhabit any structure" (*SE,* p. 178). His prose reflects his uncertainties: people, he continues, "represent, in themselves, the structure which art . . . Put it this way: If we don't cling to the warmth which breathes into a house or a poem alike from human need . . . the whole matter has nothing to hold it together and becomes structurally weak" (*SE,* p. 178).

The first ellipsis in the above quotation is Williams's, and it seems to indicate his unwillingness or inability to say what the structure of art has to do with the structure of people. The logical way to complete the sentence would be to suggest, as Williams's "Young Sycamore" suggests, that art also represents or repeats or, perhaps, objectifies the structure found in men. Such a conclusion, however, does not locate men as the origin of the essence or life which inhabits structures like plants as well as poems and buildings. Hence, Williams falters and proposes instead that all inventions arise from human need—a proposal which ignores the more radical implications of his poetics and yet still, as we have seen, begs the question of how, in the practical American context Williams sets himself, one might show that poetry is important and necessary.

Williams, in 1944, cautions that the "arts have a *complex* relation to society" (*SE*, p. 256). Exploring one aspect of his attempts to define this relation illuminates the development of Williams's poetry and poetics. More importantly, though, Williams, in adopting a modern style commonly associated with the rise of technology, and in simultaneously attempting an analysis of American modernity generally, reveals the difficulties involved in sustaining a defense of modern poetry or in describing its importance, given the apparent needs of the modern world.

IV

I have mentioned that Williams describes his first attraction to what I have been calling a machine aesthetic as due in part to his desire to be allied with various avant-garde movements in a number of the arts. The same desire seems to have fed his willingness to experiment with other styles and theories associated with modernism, some of which coexist uneasily with the style and poetics just discussed. Williams's attempts to outline the nature and importance of a different kind of poetry cast light upon the endeavors of modernists in a number of fields, and upon the sometimes contradictory poetics identified as modernist. Further, Williams's thought again reveals the importance of the relationship between science and the arts to the modernist project.

Williams's more fluid style, which he says he "liked to do most of all,"[22] is evidenced in *Kora in Hell,* as well as in the later "The Sea-Elephant" and "The Trees" (to pick poems which differ obviously from poems like "Young Sycamore"). The analogues proposed for this fluid style, both by Williams and by his critics, are many, including Dadaist and Surrealist experiments in the plastic arts, Bergson's philosophy, and, most surprisingly perhaps, the creative and natural energy at the root of scientific advances, an energy which, in "Young Sycamore," seems to be defined structurally.[23]

Williams's claim that poetry reveals a universal presence seems to remain constant, but his characterization of the nature of that presence changes, both explicitly and implicitly, in his defense of a fluid style. For example, when Williams calls for "the authentic spirit of change" (*I*, p. 13) or for a "loosen[ing of] the attention" (*I*, p. 14) in *Kora in Hell*, the style of that poem—almost a stream of consciousness—calls attention to a nearly manic energy which one is invited to see as an expression of inner character, of the imagination at work (or at play). This characterization of imaginative energy does not insist upon the hard-edged, sparse style which Williams elsewhere defends. Indeed, he says of Sheeler's Precisionist photographic lines, "someone should smash his camera and open his brain,"[24] a charge which indicates Williams's suspicions that his own experiments with a machine style might not adequately emphasize—or accurately characterize—the creative activity he so often celebrates and which he identifies as central to his defense of modern poetry.

In poems such as those entitled "Della Primavera Trasportata al Morale," one can see Williams associating mental activity with a loosened style and with the images of radiance, heat, and light in terms of which he frequently discusses "the radiant gist" (*P*, p. 186) revealed by, or released by, poetry. In the title poem ("Della Primavera Trasportata al Morale"), Williams offers as his "moral[s]": "it looses me" and "it has never ceased / to flow" (*CEP*, p. 59). The poem concludes in a familiar vein, announcing that the "forms / of the emotions are crystalline, / geometric-faceted"; however, the style of the poem mimics the "white heat of / understanding, when a flame / runs through the gap made / by learning" (*CEP*, p. 64). The gap, presumably, is similar to Stevens's "dumbfoundering abyss / Between us and the object,"[25] a gap Williams fills between crystalline objects and crystalline emotions by the flame of the creative imagination in motion. Finally, the poem as a whole, largely because of its style, concentrates less upon structure than upon fluidity or motion as the basic characteristic of creative understanding and as the key to the importance of poems which call attention to the much needed play of imagination.

Mike Weaver describes Williams's growing concern with motion in the thirties and convincingly argues that Williams draws on current discussions of relativity and, after 1926, on Whitehead's *Science and the Modern World* in formulating a new poetics.[26] While I agree that the new science, particularly Einsteinian physics, plays an important role in Williams's defense of a fluid style and, as I shall propose, in Williams's eventual reconciliation of his two styles in his mature poetics, I would like to complicate the question of the influence of science on Williams.

It is important to note that Williams's concern with motion, evidenced in the style of *Kora in Hell*, predates his exposure to the new science and seems to owe as much to the Surrealists or to Bergson—that is, to modernist poetics generally—as to Whitehead. It is not until 1927 that Williams's discussions with Riorden properly introduce him to the new physics, and it is not until later in the same year that Williams, reading Whitehead, pronounces *Science and the Modern World* a "milestone" in his career.[27] His statement suggests that Williams had not previously seen exactly how the new physics might be relevant to his poetics.

Einstein and the Curies do appear in Williams's early writings, not surprisingly, since by 1921 the *New Republic* was editorializing about them as "fads" (20 July 1921, p. 206).[28] I am suggesting, however, that early images of Einstein and of motion in Williams probably draw in large part on the common misconception that "the theory of relativity demands a Bergsonian philosophy," a notion Morris Cohen deplores finding in at least one of the eleven books on the new physics he reviews in 1921.[29] In short, Einsteinian physics received more publicity than understanding. Given also the popular conflation of science and technology, Williams's early view of Einstein is better seen in light of his general ambivalence about science and technology than in light of Einstein's actual theories.

Still, examining the image of Einstein in Williams's writing before 1927 does yield interesting results. Einstein appears in early issues of *Contact* and in the 1921 "St. Francis Einstein of the Daffodils,"[30] which prefigures both *In the American Grain* and, more importantly for the point I wish to make about the continuity of Williams's experiments with a fluid style, "Della Primavera Trasportata al Morale." Not only are images of a new beauty and spring juxtaposed with images of urban slums and American commercialism in both poems, but the "top-branches / [swaying] with contrary motions" of "St. Francis Einstein" become "the tree moving diversely / in all parts" (*CEP*, p. 60) in the later poem. Both poems set the eccentric twigs of "Young Sycamore" in motion, imagistically and stylistically, and both suggest that style will be an important part of Williams's portrayal of motion or underlying energy.

In 1921, it seems that Williams has Einstein preside over his fluid style in part because of the connection popularly drawn between relativity theory and a universe of flux. Einstein is further called upon to defend the artists' mental flux, or the constant dismantling of old forms in order to create anew, commonly associated with modernist poetics and what I have called a fluid style. The extension of the idea of relativity to the inner as well as the outer world also insists upon the identification of Einstein's constant—the speed of light—with a dynamic motion, already in Williams imaged as light or flame in motion. In other words, already existing notions of an inner motion as a universal human essence come to be associated with Einstein.

For Williams, constant creation is associated specifically with the ongoing production of language in poetry. Thus, in the January 1921 issue of *Contact,* St. Francis—a figure dubbed St. Francis Einstein in the next issue of *Contact*—is the saint of communication. St. Francis, says Williams, finds "a common stem where all [are] one and from which every paired characteristic branch[es]" (*SE*, p. 28). Here, as in "Della Primavera Trasportata al Morale," one finds creative activity emphasized and imaged not as the formal dualism, the horned twigs, of "Young Sycamore," but as that which joins the forked branches, as Einstein's constant moving freely from object to object, providing the medium by which all things are related.

Williams's early use of Einstein, then, seeks a scientific foundation for a poetics which Williams and others had begun to develop well before Einstein's public appearance. As with technological advances, Einstein seems to offer a definition of the modern which, along with his popularity and the scientific "truth" of his theories, might easily be appropriated for poetry. Moreover—although, ironically, it seems only a confusion of science with technology would lead to the canonization of St. Francis, and so of Einstein, as "the patron saint of *the United States*" (*SE*, p. 27; emphasis added)—the popularity of Einsteinian physics seems to offer the proof Williams wants that

Americans can admire and find a place for a creative intelligence, the results of which are not measured commercially. The uses of the arts and of relativity theory, at least in 1921, are more easily compared than the uses of poetry and of bathroom or kitchen fixtures. Finally, Einstein's primary characteristic for Williams in 1921 seems to be the fact that he offers a new vision of the world, just as Williams would have poetry do.

In short, Einstein seems to provide just the image Williams needs of how American science, although not exactly the "science" on which America prided itself, could define the place of modernist art in modern society, offering a different, and in ways less problematic, analogy between science and art than does technological science. At the same time, however, Williams displays some anxiety about allowing scientific truths to underwrite his poetry. Despite his and others' equation of science and poetry, the papers were not inclined to grant visiting artists the same enthusiastic reception that they granted Einstein. Thus, Williams wavers between claiming Einstein for poetry, claiming poetry's superiority to science, and casting doubt on the reasons for Einstein's popularity.

One can see Williams's defensiveness about Einstein best, perhaps, in his essays. The press provides the suggestion, echoed by Williams, that Einstein is merely a follower. The *Nation* of 27 December 1919 proclaims: "Religion and poetry, of course, have always known that space and time are relative" (p. 819). Similarly, Williams's 1934 polemic says that scientists "haven't understood that one plus one plus one plus one plus one equals not five but one," and yet hastens to add that "even science is beginning at last to catch on to it";[31] that is, science will validate poetry, but poetry first discovered scientific truths. To return to Williams's statements in 1921, St. Francis Einstein is the saint of communication and of process, but sainthood is a questionable status: "A patron saint is one thing but in the intercommunications of art there should be something more" (*SE*, p. 27). Poetry, Williams goes on to suggest, will be not equivalent to science, but rather more relevant to society.

Given Williams's ambivalence about science in the essays, it is not surprising that Williams's first poem about Einstein displays the same mixed tone. In "St. Francis Einstein of the Daffodils," one finds Einstein in back of the cycles of change that originate in *Kora in Hell*. Einstein—a familiar, if not easily visualized, combination of Columbus, Venus, and Spring—arrives in the new world and frees it from classical notions of beauty, from the past. He is not only observed from several frames of reference, as Carol Donley suggests,[32] but he brings both creation and destruction, presiding over an old negro who invites cats (including Lesbia's black cat) to eat poison fish. The juxtapositions are, initially, characteristic of Williams's insistence on change: southerly winds follow northerly gales; creation follows destruction; to leave us with the motions of awakening and uncovering.

Yet, though the poem's style reinforces our sense of motion and fluidity, Williams mockingly presents it as his newest product, prefacing what he calls a "sample poem" with the announcement that a "minimum price of fifty dollars will be charged for all poems, those of most excellence, as in all commercial exchange, being rated higher in price," adding that the gauge of excellence will be "length and success" (p. 2). The bitterness of this opening seems called forth by Einstein's success in America; and in the poem itself one finds a similar tone. Einstein arrives "to *buy* freedom / for the daffodils" (emphasis added) and he arrives "in fashion" as the "wise newspapers / . . . quote the great mathematician." The sarcasm is evident, as is Williams's uneasiness with Einstein's popularity, which he links with the commercial success of technology, even as he claims Einstein's theories for poetry. In *The Embodiment of Knowledge* Williams has a somewhat confusing set of notes on the European modernists' successful predictions of war, followed by some comments on Lewis's criticism of Pound. He ends this discussion with a stutter which underlines his own confusion: "we are convinced by this pander because, by God, what he says is scientifically and scientifically [*sic*] true. We buy his book" (*EK*, p. 84). What Pound's book, or Lewis's criticisms of Pound, have to do with science—or with the accuracy of literary predictions—is unclear. What is clear is that the image of prostituting oneself is tied to the commercial and popular success of those books which can be called "scientifically true." While Williams does wish to show that poetry is as "true" and as important as science, he wishes also to rescue poetry from the necessity of competing with science for the truth. This is in part due to his sense that scientific truths do have commercial value while poetic truths do not.

In the course of his rescue mission, Williams also offers a plea that theoretical science not be made subservient to technological or commercial demands. "St. Francis Einstein of the Daffodils" seems to begin a serious critique of the temptations to

which theoretical science is prey, a critique developed more
fully in *In the American Grain*. Einstein, in the early poem, positively affirms the necessity of theoretical intelligence, while
sharing with art, and with America generally, the destruction
entailed by true creativity. But the poison fish-heads said to be
described by Einstein's mathematics in the poem are an image
of destruction which Williams elsewhere disassociates from necessary destruction. In *In the American Grain*, Williams has Columbus (a figure for Einstein in "St. Francis Einstein") discover
diverse trees, strange fish (*IAG*, p. 26) and an "acrid and
poisonous apple" (*IAG*, p. 7). Although neither *In the American
Grain* nor "St. Francis Einstein" uncovers a snake in the garden,
a late essay on Sandburg identifies theoretical intelligence as
"the active worm in the fruit" (*SE*, p. 273), mixing the images of
snakes, worms, and apples. All images of the necessary evil in
paradise are associated with the destruction that Williams insists must accompany creation, to make room for yet newer
creations.

   In this context, it is significant that Williams calls both scientists and saints "snake charmers" (*IAG*, p. 207), and that he
venomously remarks on how the "mysterious is so simple when
revealed by science," after quoting from a pedantic explanation
of how the "fiery serpent that bit the children of Israel when
they wandered through the wilderness was possibly the guinea
worm" (*IAG*, pp. 222–23). Williams's point seems to be that the
creative intelligence of scientists (snake charmers) is too domes-
ticated,[33] as with Einstein, too prone to accept commercial and
popular support for its products and thus to accept easy answers. Certainly this is Williams's point when, later, he discusses
the war, and complains that "the true nature of the revolutionary St. Francis—whom they recaptured and subjected to
their rule"—is the nature of "the running animal" (*SE*, p. 246).

   On one hand, Williams applauds the validity and the respect
granted to the "true" Einstein, criticizing only the domes-
tication of science. On the other hand, Williams insists that
poetry already has the virtues but not the vices of science, ig-
noring his own somewhat jealous recognition elsewhere that
poetry's *temptations* are not those of science. It is worth pausing
to notice that Einstein's importance to Williams's modernist poetics, like the importance of contemporary technological developments, grows out of the need, which Williams shows in his
early writings, to discover what the arts have to offer in an age
dominated by science and technology. Williams's analogies be-

tween poetry and physics, then, like his analogies between poetry and technology, are not straightforward (or even confused) reflections of specific contemporary developments so much as an attempt to solve the general problem of how the arts might be related to, without being subsumed by, the sciences. Williams's uneasiness about his debt to Einstein thus testifies more eloquently than the debt itself to his modernity.

Williams's use of Einstein's ideas changes after his exposure to less popularized versions of the new science. It is beyond the purpose of this paper to trace with any detail the development of Williams's thoughts on relativity theory and measurement or his related interest in the Curies' work on radium.[34] I would like to propose, however, that Einstein, in particular, continues to be of central importance to Williams's poetics because his theories, as Williams comes to understand them, serve to reconcile the poetics of structure and the poetics of process for Williams, and thus help him forge a unified poetics and a stronger defense of poetry.

Before offering a brief sketch of how Williams uses Einsteinian physics to reconcile his two styles, let me add that Williams's ambivalence as to whether science underlines the importance of modern poetry or eclipses poetry persists throughout his career. Thus, I would argue that any consideration of Williams's later use of Einstein needs still to take into account why Einstein is important to Williams and why Williams is so nervous about claiming Einstein. For example, in his notes for an address to the University of Washington given in 1950, Williams sarcastically proclaims himself "just a literary guy, not *practical*—like a one-time atomic physicist," adding, "What a nerve to come to a going institution of learning to teach you how to write?! Even to sell? Why, you might as well have an Einstein. HE at least can play the violin" (*SE*, p. 298). The dash makes the syntax here confusing. Is Einstein more practical than Williams and a commercial success for the wrong reasons, or is he comparable to Williams ("just a literary guy, not practical") with only the slim advantage of being known to play the violin, as Williams withholds the fact that he too was an amateur violinist? The ambiguous image of the physicist-musician seems to ask the reader to look past the negative image of an overly successful scientist to see the "ultimate Einstein," who is really Williams, claiming for himself the validity and appeal he too finds in Einstein. It seems reasonable to suggest, in light of such passages, that Williams appropriates Einstein's ideas in order to reconcile his two styles—finding the "profound language, underlying all the dialectics" (A, p. 361)—with similarly mixed motives.

In adopting Einstein as the patron saint of his fluid style, Williams does not abandon his thoughts on structure or on objects. But he adds to his ideas on structure ideas gained from Einstein and Whitehead. "The Poem as a Field of Action" reviews the simple use of technological images in poetry, and sees "the new physics taking its [i.e., industrial science's] place" (SE, p. 282). As shown, however, Williams's use of industry was never simple, and in his mature poetics the new physics may be said to have subsumed both technology and physics rather than replacing one with the other. That is, the new science, especially as taken from Whitehead, proposes (as Cohen reported even in 1921) that reality, including objects, is "a flow of events,"[35] that there is no discrepancy between a celebration of process and an attention to structure or even between science and poetry. Hartley's attempt to seize "the mysticity of the moment"—the interrelatedness of things—which informed Kora in Hell is an attempt now sanctioned by the new science and shown not to be opposed to the clarity or focus of scientists or to the hard-edged lines of the Precisionists' art.[36]

The mixed style of "Della Primavera Trasportata al Morale" (in which typographical emblems, menus, and road signs are held together in a stream-of-consciousness narrative which anticipates Paterson) seems already to rest on Williams's new vision of how physics dictates a style in which disparate, apparently discrete things (being, as it were, space-time smears) coalesce in unique events. "The Sea-Elephant," for instance, part of the "Primavera" group, mocks those who would isolate objects—here the sea-elephant—or who would distort the animal which can be known only in its context of enormous flux, the sea. Interestingly, this knowledge of the animal's proper place is voiced by someone "practical": theoretical science, poetry, and the American respect for objects finally concur. As a sea creature, of course, the sea-elephant cannot be understood; his natural language—"Blouaugh!"—cannot be interpreted. Indeed, the narrative glosses are as suspect as any other voice presented in the poem; more so, perhaps, in that the lines tend to be in overly "poetic" language, as in the lines "my / flesh is riven" (CEP, p. 71). What the creature requires is

St. Francis's common stem, some way of being seen or expressed in its natural context without being converted, as Williams puts it (*SE*, p. 29).

The style of the poem provides just such a context. Although we are given mostly misinterpretations of the animal, Williams, unlike those who see only one distorted facet of the sea-elephant, has his mixed voices and rapid transitions, including several puns, hold the object as "playfully" (*CEP*, p. 73) as the sea, identifying the animal seen in its proper, multiple context as love, just as he will say that relativity is "like love" (*SE*, p. 283), a glue by which everything is interrelated.[37]

This marriage of object and process is explicitly related to physics in a number of Williams's late essays. His 1948 speech, for instance, alludes several times to Wilson's 1931 chapter on Proust, in which Wilson writes that "the ultimate units of his [the relativist's] reality are 'events,' each of which is unique" (although all are "interdependent," as indeed all fields of knowledge are interdependent).[38] Williams takes from Wilson, and from Whitehead, two further points: first, that there can be "a possible relationship—between a style and a natural science" (*SE*, p. 287)—and, second, that everything "in the social, economic complex of the world at any time-sector ties in together" (*SE*, p. 283). Thus, science and poetry are analogous, and Einsteinian physics can underwrite not only Williams's mature style, but his appropriation of science.

There is, of course, a sleight of hand involved in such reasoning. My point has been that Williams and other modernists require a sleight of hand in order to write and defend poetry in the modern world, and there is at least a poetic justice involved in having Einstein and Whitehead finally sanction Williams's reconciliation, in the late twenties, of two seemingly contradictory modernist impulses. Williams, indeed, stops writing poetry in the period preceding the appearance of the poems I have identified as reconciling his two earlier styles, offering as an explanation: "the form has been lacking" (*SL*, p. 129). He emerges from a period of silence with a style approved by science, yet which he can claim as having been first the province of poets.[39]

Williams's attempt to forge a coherent poetics in the particular modern context to which he, uniquely, paid such close attention reveals both the importance and the difficulty of his project. If his defense of poetry is sometimes confused or confusing, the very terms of his confusion provide the mirror to modernity in search of which he began his career. Further-more, the problems Williams raises and the questions he asks are still very much with us, in part because of him: Williams is not only, to quote from Lionel Trilling's discussion of literary history, to "be used as [a] barometer . . . he is also part of the weather."[40]

1. Citations from Williams will be noted in my text as follows:

A   *The Autobiography of William Carlos Williams* (New York: New Directions, 1967).
CEP   *The Collected Earlier Poems* (1951; rpt. New York: New Directions,1966).
CLP   *The Collected Later Poems*, rev. ed. (1963; rpt. New York: New Directions, 1967).
EK   *The Embodiment of Knowledge* (New York: New Directions, 1974).
I   *Imaginations* (New York: New Directions, 1970).
IAG   *In the American Grain*, rev. ed. (New York: New Directions, 1966).
L   *The Selected Letters of William Carlos Williams*, ed. John C. Thirlwall (New York: McDowell, Obolensky, 1957).
SE   *Selected Essays of William Carlos Williams* (New York: Random House, 1954).
SSA   *Interviews with William Carlos Williams: "Speaking Straight Ahead,"* ed. Linda Wagner (New York: New Directions, 1976).
P   *Paterson* (New York: New Directions, 1963).

2. Discussions of Williams's fascination with modern art are numerous. For the most extended considerations of the topic, see Bram Dijkstra, *The Hieroglyphics of a New Speech: Cubism, Stieglitz, and the Early Poetry of William Carlos Williams* (Princeton, N.J.: Princeton University Press, 1969); Dickran Tashjian, *Skyscraper Primitives: Dada and the American Avant-Garde, 1910–1925* (Middletown, Conn.: Wesleyan University Press, 1975); idem, *William Carlos Williams and the American Scene, 1920–1940* (New York: Whitney Museum of American Art, 1978), and Williams's own statements in *A Recognizable Image: William Carlos Williams on Art and Artists*, ed. Bram Dijkstra (New York: New Directions, 1978). Tashjian and Mike Weaver, *William Carlos Williams: The American Background* (Cambridge: Cambridge University Press, 1971) provide the most comprehensive notes on general influences on Williams, while Carol C. Donley's article, "Relativity and Radioactivity in William Carlos Williams' *Paterson*," *William Carlos Williams Newsletter* 5, no. 1 (Spring 1979): 6–11, cites most of the papers, articles, and theses which show the rising interest in Williams's relationship to science.

3. Williams's association with *The Seven Arts* is well documented: see, for instance, Dijkstra, *The Hieroglyphics of a New Speech*, pp. 42 and 108. Williams himself mentions both *The Seven Arts* (A, p. 147) and *The Blind Man* (I, p. 10), as well as commenting specifically on Duchamp's "Fountain" (A, p. 134).

4. For a discussion of the long history behind these thoughts on the relationship between technology and art in America, see John F. Kasson, "Technology and Imaginative Freedom: R. W. Emerson" and "The Aesthetics of Machinery," *Civilizing the Machine: Technology and Republican Values in America, 1776–1900* (New York: Grossman-Viking, 1976), pp. 107–80.

5. Lewis Mumford, *American Taste* (San Francisco: The Westgate Press, 1929), p. 25.

6. Wallace Stevens, *Opus Posthumous*, ed. Samuel French Morse (1957; rpt. New York: Alfred A. Knopf, 1972), p. 216.

7. As mentioned above, critics often refer these stylistic experiments to the work and theories of Pound, in his Imagist phase, or to the painters of the Arensberg circle.

8. A sometimes qualified optimism and a concern with the social role of poetry occurs frequently in American modernist poets: there is Moore's acknowledgment, in "Poetry," that although "there are things that are important beyond all this fiddle," there is something "important" and "useful" in poetry (Marianne Moore, *Collected Poems* [New York: MacMillan, 1951], pp. 40–41); Stevens's insistence that poetry helps "people to live their lives" (*The Necessary Angel* [New York: Vintage-Random House, 1951], p. 29); and Williams's late claim that, although it "is difficult / to get the news from poems / . . . men die miserably every day / for lack / of what is found there" (*Pictures from Brueghel and other poems* [1962; rpt. New York: New Directions, 1967], pp. 161–62). The causes of this optimism are clearly more complex than Stein, in citing technology, suggests. It is enough for my purposes here, however, to note that Stein's suggestion is made in 1917, revealing a contemporary analysis of the sources of the American character. For a more careful study, see Henry F. May, *The End of American Innocence* (1959; rpt. Chicago: Quadrangle Books, 1964) on "practical idealism." Last, it is appropriate to note here Pound's remarks to Williams: "The thing that saves your work is *opacity* . . . NOT an American quality." *The Letters of Ezra Pound*, ed. D. D. Page (New York: Harcourt, Brace and World, 1950), p. 12.

9. See Tashjian, *Skyscraper Primitives*, pp. 87ff., for a brief but insightful discussion of this passage as relating Williams to the theories of the European modernists, the Dadaists in particular, even as Williams attempts to define an American context for art. As Tashjian remarks, Williams's "reasoning generated certain tensions" (p. 87). Williams's definition of inventive intelligence, which he insists on appropriating for America, owes a debt not only to Dada, but to ideas being formulated in a number of other artistic circles: Stravinsky, for instance, distinguishes between imagination or fantasy and "invention [which] is not conceivable apart from actual working-out." *Poetics of Music* (1947; rpt. New York: Vintage Books, 1956), p. 53.

10. Here, as elsewhere, I have not discussed the way in which Williams takes the urban, industrial landscape as his main *subject*, but one should see James E. Breslin, *William Carlos Williams: An American Artist* (New York: Oxford University Press, 1970), pp. 66–68, for a suggestion on how, in poems like "At the Faucet of June," Williams criticizes industrialists, while taking from them an ideal of beauty. See also poems like "View of a Lake" (*CEP*, p. 96) and *In the American Grain*, pp. 68 and 128.

11. *The Seven Arts*'s notorious antiwar stand usually made it a unique forum, in 1917, for debates on the *abuses* of technology and science. More often, science and technology were viewed positively. Indeed, the image of the creativity of the scientist is not limited to discussions of theoretical science in relatively "highbrow" magazines like *The Seven Arts* or to avant-garde films such as L'Herbiers's (1923) *L'Inhumaine*, shown in New York together with Leger's *Ballet Mécanique* (which it inspired) in 1926—when Williams saw it (Weaver, p. 69). Cf. S. D. Lawder, *The Cubist Cinema* (New York: New York University Press, 1975). The hero of the early-thirties movie *I Am a Fugitive from a Chain Gang*, discussed by Andrew Bergman, *We're in the Money* (1971; rpt. New York: Harper Colophon, 1972), returns home from the war saying that he wants "to get away from routine . . . and create" (Bergman, p. 94) by becoming an engineer.

12. See also Williams's earlier dismissal of simple characterizations of the "Utilization of Knowledge," where he insists that scientific knowledge is not to be humanized: "It is human, *purely*" (*EK*, p. 83; emphasis added).

13. See, for instance, the statement that "knowledge itself is . . . a machine" (*EK*, p. 63).

14. As Lionel Trilling notes, both history and literary studies in this era learned "that

in an age of science prestige is to be gained by approximating the methods of science." "The Sense of the Past," in *Influx: Essays on Literary Influence*, ed. Ronald Primeau (Port Washington, N.Y.: Kennikat Press, 1977), p. 23.

15. Introduction, *William Carlos Williams: A Collection of Critical Essays*, ed. J. Hillis Miller (Englewood Cliffs, N.J.: Prentice-Hall, 1966), p. 12. Thus, the poem is not meant to provide us with a new way of looking at trees. Indeed, as Dijkstra points out, the poem may be inspired by a work of art: Stieglitz's photograph "Spring Showers" (*The Hieroglyphics of a New Speech*, p. 190).

16. Miller, pp. 3 and 8, describes the tree as nonsymbolic, but goes on to note that "Young Sycamore" exemplifies Williams's most characteristic mode of describing motion. See also Richard A. Macksey, "'A Certainty of Music': Williams' Changes," in Miller, pp. 132–47, and J. Hillis Miller, *Poets of Reality: Six Twentieth-Century Writers* (New York: Atheneum, 1969), pp. 328–55, on Williams's "cycles."

17. Indeed, the trunk's "undulant / thrust" is recalled by Williams's description of the "undulant" character of both poems and machines in the 1944 introduction to *The Wedge* (*SE*, p. 256).

18. See Williams's statement that "the coining of similes is a pastime of very low order" (*I*, p. 18).

19. Williams describes Sheeler's later art as "subtler particularization, the *abstract* if you will" (*SE*, p. 233; emphasis added).

20. *Selected Prose of T. S. Eliot*, ed. Frank Kermode (New York: Farrar, Straus, and Giroux, 1975), p. 40. Obviously, I have ignored the complexity of Eliot's discussion of the artist's extinction of personality, in order to make my point about the common association between personality and science. I could equally well have invoked others, for example, Auden, whose rebuke to Spender for his love of classical music goes as follows: "the poet's attitude must be absolutely detached, like that of a surgeon or scientist." Cited by Julian Symons, *The Thirties: A Dream Revolved* (London: The Cresset Press, 1960), p. 13.

21. Rod Townley, *The Early Poetry of William Carlos Williams* (1972; rpt. Ithaca, N.Y.: Cornell University Press, 1975), p. 147, quotes the following from "Belly Music" (*Others* 5 [July 1919]: 26): "Poets have written of the big leaves and the little leaves, leaves that are red, green, yellow and the one thing they have never seen about a leaf is that it is a little engine. It is one of the things that make a plant GO."

22. Letter to Jim Higgins, undated, cited by Weaver, *William Carlos Williams: The American Background*, p. 42.

23. See, for discussions of Williams's fluid style, Breslin, *William Carlos Williams: An American Artist*, pp. 34–35; Townley, *The Early Poetry*, pp. 155–56, and Reed Whittemore, *William Carlos Williams: Poet from Jersey* (Boston: Houghton Mifflin Company, 1975), p. 122. For passing references to modernist analogies between the fluid style and current scientific theories, see Hugh Kenner, *The Pound Era* (Berkeley, Calif.: University of California Press, 1971), p. 153 and Whittemore, pp. 115–16. See also Joseph N. Riddel, *The Inverted Bell: Modernism and the Counterpoetics of William Carlos Williams* (Baton Rouge, La.: Louisiana State University Press, 1974), pp. 235–36, for associations between Einstein and structurally defined "essences."

24. Letter to Constance Rourke, 10 January 1938 (copy in the Yale Collection), cited by Weaver, p. 62.

25. Wallace Stevens, *The Collected Poems* (1954; rpt. New York: Knopf, 1973), p. 437.

26. Weaver, pp. 47–48, 65–66, 70.

27. Williams's letter on *Science and the Modern World* is cited by Weaver, p. 48.

28. See Carol C. Donley's account of popular press coverage of Einstein in "'A little touch of / Einstein in the night—': Williams' Early Exposure to the Theories of Relativ-

ity," *William Carlos Williams Newsletter* 4, no. 1 (Spring 1978): 10–13. Obviously, I do not agree with Donley's implicit suggestion of how Williams understood relativity theory between 1919 and 1926 or with her suggestion that Williams welcomed Einstein whole-heartedly.

29. Morris R. Cohen, "Roads to Einstein," *New Republic*, 6 July 1921, p. 174.

30. All references will be to the early version of the poem found in *Contact*, no. 4 (Summer 1921), pp. 2–4.

31. "Reply to a Young Scientist Berating Me Because of My Devotion to a Matter of Words," *Direction* 1 (Autumn 1934): 28. Note Williams's pun on "matter."

32. Donley, "A little touch of / Einstein," p. 12.

33. In "Reply to a Young Scientist," in fact, Williams calls scientists not only "learned dumb-bell[s]" but "poor fishes" (p. 28), recalling the poisonous fish of "St. Francis Einstein."

34. Williams's late fascination with science has, as many of my notes here acknowl-edge, been noted at least in passing by numerous critical studies. The implications of his scientific language have only recently been questioned, though the MLA Special Ses-sion on "William Carlos Williams and Science," in New York, December 1978, shows the growing critical interest in exploring this topic further. The program for the 1978 session is printed in the *William Carlos Williams Newsletter* 4, no. 1 (Spring 1978): 26. With the exception of Donley's "A little touch of / Einstein," most recent studies have concentrated on very late works of Williams.

35. Cohen, "Roads to Einstein," p. 174.

36. Hartley's letter to Stieglitz of June 1915 (in the Yale Collection) is cited by Weaver, p. 42, as an important influence on Williams's experiments in *Kora in Hell*.

37. Thus the "Primavera" group, including "The Sea-Elephant," is not a throwback to early experiments, unrelated to the poems more immediately preceding it, as Town-ley suggests (p. 156). Rather, the poems take Williams's fluid style as a way of emphasiz-ing both motion and attention to the particular, incorporating into the poems some of the features found in poems like "Young Sycamore."

38. Edmund Wilson, *Axel's Castle* (New York: Charles Scribner's Sons, 1931), pp. 157–58.

39. Williams's need to reconcile his two styles grows out of more than the necessity that poetry provide a coherent account of itself to a skeptical world (a world of which the poets were part). For instance, Malcolm Bradbury's and James McFarlane's study— not primarily on American modernism—notes the *"bifurcation"* of the impulse to be modern" and suggests that the best characterization of the modernist project generally might be the fusion or "juxtaposing of contradictions for resolution." "The Name and Nature of Modernism," in *Modernism*, ed. Bradbury and McFarlane (Harmondsworth: Penguin Books, 1976), pp. 44 and 48. Bradbury and McFarlane focus on the tensions between Classicism and Romanticism. My point is not that the rapid growth of science and technology is the only factor involved in the poets' need for, and difficulty in finding, a coherent defense of poetry, but that in focusing on science and technology, Williams helps reveal an important and often ignored pressure on the modernists, one to which their own choice of images and metaphors calls attention. The crisis that Williams, like Stevens and Moore, undergoes in the thirties is obviously related most immediately to the Depression. Nonetheless, I would argue that the Depression merely underlined the already sensitive issue of the problematic role of the arts in society.

40. Trilling, "The Sense of the Past," in *Influx*, p. 29.

Pattern, Concrete, and Computer Poetry: The Poem as Object in Itself

Kenneth B. Newell

Christopher Newport College

PATTERN, Concrete, and Computer poetry constitute a sequence of development. They are three distinct species in the continuing evolution of the influence of technology on poetry. By this evolution, I do not mean that Concrete grew solely out of Pattern poetry or that Computer grew out of Concrete poetry at all. Pattern is only one of many progenitors of Concrete poetry (some others are the ideogram, concrete painting, montage technique, *Ulysses*, and *Finnegans Wake*), and Concrete is not even a progenitor of Computer poetry. The latter grew out of efforts, by programmers and linguists interested in data manipulation and artificial intelligence, to experiment with random sentence generation. Consequently, all three types of poetry are results or offshoots of evolving technology as it has influenced poetry. In terms of a "family tree," the three types of poetry would represent three successive children of a long-lived parent (evolving technology) rather than parent, child, and grandchild respectively.

The influence of technology on poetry began even with the invention of the first writing implement and the first material capable of being written on. Poetry, which before these inventions could be only spoken and heard, could afterwards be written by the hand and read by the eye. The technology of writing freed poetry from restriction to the memorizable and the pronounceable and altered its form and development. The

159

poem now had *visible* form and so could then, in a succeeding stage, be given *visual* form as well: it could be shaped into a visual pattern. This happened, supposedly, in Greek Alexandria about 300 B.C.—when the earliest extant pattern poems were written—or, rather, shaped. Typical examples of this genre outline a recognizable picture to the reader's eye by means of the position and length of each line and stanza on the page. The picture formed may be a geometric design, a silhouette of an object, or an abstract visual representation of moods and ideas expressed in the poem. In the best examples of the genre, the pattern gives such an appropriate visual dimension to those moods and ideas that, if the pattern were absent, expression of them would seem less rich. The pattern complements rather than supplements the verbal expression— for the two together make a poetic whole, even though the verbal expression would still make sense if the pattern were removed and the poem were recast into traditional typographic shape.

The practice of writing pattern poems was never widespread in the ancient world and seems to have been confined to one small school in Alexandria, but later the practice was taken up in Europe by medieval Latinists and in Asia by Hindu pundits and Persian courtiers. Then, evolving technology again influenced poetry by the invention of small type and the printing press, and when pattern poetry was imported from Persia into Renaissance England the invention of printing made patterning not only easier but visually commanding; the genre appealed to reputable poets of the time and became widely known. Francis Quarles, George Wither, Robert Herrick, Thomas Traherne, and George Herbert indulged in composing in the genre. Unfortunately, too many lesser poets also indulged; they earned the scorn of critics and soon brought pattern poetry into disrepute and disuse. However, it appeared again in the nineteenth century and was unashamedly composed in the twentieth by Guillaume Apollinaire, Hart Crane, and Dylan Thomas. Indeed, like George Herbert, Apollinaire and Thomas raised Pattern poetry to the level of high art.

Also in the late nineteenth and twentieth century the invention of the modern typewriter and the further development of printing encouraged an additional way to pattern poems. Instead of giving them *outer* shape or outline by manipulating position and length of line and stanza, some poets gave them *inner* shape by manipulating the spacing and position of letters, words, and phrases within the line and by using unconventional typographic variations and notations. Apollinaire did this too, and so did Mallarmé, Pound, Cummings, and William Carlos Williams.[1]

It is partly from this practice and from these practitioners that some poets in the middle 1950s took inspiration and launched the Concrete poetry movement. In this kind of poetry, the spacing, position, and typographical peculiarities of letters, words, and phrases on the page became the *principal*—sometimes the only—mode of expression. Concrete differs from Pattern poetry in that the verbal expression in Concrete would usually not make sense without the visual presentation, but not always—for some Concrete poems are designed to be read aloud and heard as well as seen. But, in the majority of cases, the visual aspect alone makes the poem. This distinct and different species of poetry evolved because poets were learning to use with creativity the typewriter and graphics-reproduction equipment—the next step in the influence of technology upon poetry.[2]

In the early 1960s the computer was put to use in composing poetry—or at least in assisting a human being in assembling word groupings that look superficially like poetry but may have to be called by some other more precise term if the practice continues. The term *Computer poetry* is less accurate than "computer-assisted poetry" or, better, "quasi poetry" to emphasize crucial distinctions between poetry that is computer-assisted and poetry that is not. These distinctions have been ably discussed by others[3] and so will not be discussed here, but the relationship between Concrete and Computer poetry will be.

In 1962 R. M. Worthy was the first to compose poetry with a computer, which he nicknamed AutoBeatnik.[4] As I specified earlier, I do not mean to imply that Worthy was able to do so because of the prior existence of the Concrete poetry movement. AutoBeatnik could poetize because the technology that had made possible Concrete poetry advanced to the point where it made possible Computer poetry. On the other hand, I would still like to emphasize the relationship between them—first, by noting that basic computer-versifying principles of permutational change, randomness, and repetition had always been common ingredients in Concrete poetry, even years before the poetizing of AutoBeatnik. Around 1917 the Dadaist Hans Arp had created "Arpaden" and "Torn Papers"—two types of proto-Concrete poems which may be considered proto-

Computer poems as well, for they incorporated "the axiom of 'the law of chance' which let things fall where they wanted."[5] The material in both the Arpaden and Torn Papers was derived from extant sources and then combined into unique assortments. For the Arpaden, Arp selected the material at random—and often with closed eyes—from daily newspapers and advertizing columns. For the Torn Papers, he tore up or apart extant written material and reassembled it differently to form new structures. "In this manner, 'reality and chance' . . . could reign supreme in their unique, unplanned coincidences" (Gumpel, p. 56). These proto-Concrete poems thus approximate the randomness of assembling elements for a Computer poem, although the latter often uses language selected or figuratively "torn" from traditional poetry instead. And, like Computer poetry

> the Arpaden and Torn Papers underscore a *heuristic* foundation for a text, since it is no longer put together solely by authorial planning but is also "guided" by the material to be manipulated. Control is thus balanced between the autonomy of *medium* and *manipulator* rather than being identified with only the semantic intent of the latter. The result thus has to be a kind of *semantic anonymity* as far as the author is concerned. . . . The objective here is esthetic, for it guarantees "the great independence of the poem from its creator." [Gumpel, pp. 56–57]

Furthermore, "Arp's 'performance' during selection converted the poetic *process* into a genuine poetic *act*"—for, according to concretist successors, it preceded verbalization, was "sufficiently impromptu to include the element of chance," and was alogical (Gumpel, p. 57).

Between 1956 and 1969, a group of Viennese concretists, unaware of the Arpaden, created poems *(verbarien)* resembling them. But the Viennese used encyclopedias rather than newspapers for their "stockpile of words" and, after selecting them at random, used them serially "to yield (vertical) textual structures" (Gumpel, p. 57).

One of the half-dozen founders of the Concrete movement, Décio Pignatari, was a specialist in information theory and computers,[6] and, four years before the appearance of AutoBeatnik, Pignatari and two other founders, the De Campos brothers, stated in a "Pilot Plan" a relationship between Concrete poetry and "cybernetics, the poem as a mechanism regulating itself."[7]

This relationship was continually reaffirmed in the years following AutoBeatnik. In 1963 the Concrete poet Edwin Morgan

The Computer's First Christmas Card

```
jollymerry
hollyberry
jollyberry
merryholly
happyjolly
jollyjelly
jellybelly
bellymerry
hollyheppy
jollyMolly
marryJerry
merryHarry
hoppyBarry
heppyJarry
boppyheppy
berryjorry
jorryjolly
moppyjelly
Mollymerry
Jerryjolly
bellyboppy
jorryhoppy
hollymoppy
Barrymerry
Jarryhappy
happyboppy
boppyjolly
jollymerry
merrymerry
merrymerry
merryChris
ammerryasa
Chrismerry
asMERRYCHR
YSANTHEMUM
```

Fig. 1

Reprinted from *Concrete Poetry: A World View*, ed. Mary Ellen Solt, 1968, by permission of the publisher, Indiana University Press.

composed the first in a series of what he called "simulated computer poems," in which he imitated a computer's "permutational" activity and the "blunders or digressions which at times arise (one would say) creatively within a computer context." The first poem, entitled "The Computer's First Christmas Card" (see Fig. 1), "makes use of an obvious formal grid in each line (two words each having consonant-vowel-double-consonant-y) and at the same time suggests that the machine is scanning a semantic as well as formal 'store' (all the words relating somehow to the context of Christmas cheer, . . . joy, parties, drinking . . .). It is a goal-seeking poem which misses its goal finally but in the process discovers (as a machine might) an acceptable equivalent (chrysanthemum as emblematic good-luck flower, also as a flower one might buy or give at Christmas-time)."[8] Also in 1963 the Concrete poet Pierre Garnier wrote a position paper for the International Movement in "Spatial" poetry and in it included what he called "cybernetic, serial, permutational" poetry along with Concrete.[9] Around this time the Concrete poet and theorist Max Bense used a scientific and methodical procedure—and often a computer—to select poetic material quantitatively. The theory behind his procedure is summarized by Gumpel:

> Linguistic, artistic, creative, and communicative occurrences (Vorgänge) are, like dice, "zufallsdurchsetzt," says Bense, meaning that they remain suffused by chance, probability, and thus qualify as "stochastic" processes, "aleatory" events. These occurrences, contrary to predetermined "physical" laws, bear different potentials for realization because they require *manipulative* human intervention. For instance, a repertoire of vocables, once gathered, can be calculated in accordance with degrees of freedom and control in distribution, gauging the "entropy" of still unstructured elements in relation to their potential of (free yet) available choices (verfügbare Wahlen), choices that lead to structured "information" as the elements become ordered through certain combinations. The resulting composition then exerts its own constraints (Zwang, Zwänge) upon the formation of the structure, thus generating a particular "communication." . . . The choice of a design is originally free but the constituents selected for that design consist of a *given* material, no less so in the case of words. That is to say, all compositional media harbor their own principle of *control,* a kind of regulative force or "cybernetic" propensity, according to Bense. He paraphrases "cybernetic" as "Steuerung" to underscore that the idiosyncrasies embodied in the compositional means virtually "steer" the person (or machine) using them since nothing, not even the most innovative idea, is created out of nothing. [Gumpel, pp. 58–59][10]

A Concrete poem created according to these principles might be thought of as a "computer" poem, whether it was created by a person alone or with the aid of a computer.

In 1964 Pignatari coauthored a manifesto for composing as Concrete poetry semiotic or code poems through the use of

```
Program  POEM I                                        Punching Instructions              Page    of
                                                        Graphic        Card form #        Identification
Programmer            Date              Punch                                              73      80

C FOR COMMENT
STATEMENT
NUMBER
       DIMENSION J (300)
       READ 100
 100   FORMAT (28H NOW YOU NEVER NOW YOU DONT //)
       SUM = ZERO
       DO 17 J = 1, N
       SUBSUM = SUM - TIGER + XRGUN3 * RGUN //
       TEMP = X(IB (I)*IS - PRAVDA * (IGUN //)
  17   PRAVDA = ERROR - ABSF(X + (IGUN // - TO/2DAY)
       CONTINUE
       FORMAT (22H SHAKE FIST FAST NACHT )
       X (IGUN + 11) = TEMP
       PRINT 20 ERROR
  20   FORMAT (E21.9)
       IF (ERROR - TEST) 21, 16, 16
  21   NEXT .                     X2=2
  16   NEXT                       KI = 1
       DIMENSION Y (400)
       DO 22 I = N, M, J
  22   PUNCH 1A, I, X(IGUN //), NEXT
  14   FORMAT (25H,2E3, I4, 25H HAVE A MINUTE LEFT TO KILL /)
 114   PAUSE
```

Fig. 2

Reprinted from *Concrete Poetry: A World View,* ed. Mary Ellen Solt, 1968, by permission of the publisher, Indiana University Press.

languages that included computer programming diagrams and computer languages.[11] Such poems were composed three years later by Carl Fernbach-Flarsheim. He calls them "poems for creative and non-creative computers," and one (see Fig. 2) he identifies as a "program for a computer poem generated by the poet in FORTRAN."[12] Here "computer poem" means "poem supposedly to be *fed into* a computer," not "poem produced by it."

What is advantageous about this type of poem is that if the poet were asked what it means he could always dodge by saying that he is not *supposed* to know: since the poem is a computer input tape, it was designed to be read and understood only by a computer and not by a human being. Of course, this answer would be half facetious since the poem is published in a book for human beings to read as a Concrete poem (and not for the computer to read as an input tape). In that case, the poet could dodge the question in the opposite direction and respond—again half facetiously—with an answer pertinent to any Concrete poem: that he intends no meaning by himself but requires the reader to supply one from associating the materials in the poem. In the words of Eugen Gomringer, another founder of the Concrete movement, the poet "leaves the task of association to the reader, who becomes a collaborator and, in a sense, the completer of the poem."[13] Because of its visual component "a Concrete text becomes a 'sample' or 'probe' *(Muster/Probe)* for a reader. The reader engages in an intellectual 'exercitium'; instead of being a passive recipient, he participates actively . . . in taking up the challenge (or . . . invitation) to make something of the text for himself. He must do this because he is not handed a finished theme into which he can project himself. . . . In short, the intervening visual component disrupts the tight relation between the encoding/decoding of the communicative process. Decoder cannot get back to encoder but remains somewhere suspended in the middle." However, this development is positive "since the reader may here freely exercise his *option* rather than fulfil the *obligation* of putting the text together in a certain way. Accordingly, the reader himself becomes a secondary encoder" (Gumpel, pp. 63–64).[14]

Both of the half-facetious answers to the question of interpretation are, of course, evasive, but they are also somewhat valid. They are part of the "play" or game basic to Concrete poetry[15] and to Pattern and Computer poetry too. Indeed, this element of play is more pervasive in each successive type of poetry. From traditional to Pattern to Concrete to Computer, the poem becomes more "an object in and by itself" and less "an interpreter of exterior objects and . . . subjective feelings";[16] therefore, the reader becomes more a collaborator with the poet in giving that object meaning, more a player in a game with the poet.

A Pattern poem only approaches being "an object in and by itself"; a Concrete poem is mostly such an object, though not completely so: "Though asyntactic, a Constellation [i.e., Concrete poem] cannot be entirely arepresentational since words, to be what they are, bear a content reflecting the extant reality" (Gumpel, p. 40).[17] On the other hand, statements of the complete arepresentationality of Concrete poetry abound among practitioners and theorists of the genre:

> A Constellation is "a reality in itself and not a poem about. . . ." [Gomringer, *worte,* his ellipsis; cited in Gumpel, p. 41]

> The goal of concretism is not to represent *(darstellen)* the "reality of experience" but rather to make something realizable, something that has no antecedent existence. [Gumpel, p. 62; paraphrase of Siegfried J. Schmidt, "Konkrete Poesie: Ergebnisse und Perspektiven."]

> The goal was not to "represent" and "reduplicate" what was already extant but rather to "present" and "produce" anew. . . . Language . . . should not be instrumental in producing another reality, but is there to exemplify the reality of language as it reveals itself. [Gumpel, pp. 43–44; paraphrase of Bense, *Aesthetica.*]

> It was not a matter of showing a "represented" world in art but rather of "representing from a world" possessing its own intrinsic reality, . . . [of performing an] activity that will produce its own world, one whose inception can only occur through art. [Gumpel, p. 44; paraphrase of Bense, "kleine abstrakte ästhetik."]

Notwithstanding, arepresentation raises the question whether a Concrete poem, if completely arepresentational, still qualifies as a sign in communication. Since "a sign is something which stands for something else, . . . what the sign stands for is *absent* from the sign. The sign stands for something that is not itself, that is missing. . . . The verbal sign is in some sense a substitution for the thing signified and can never *be* the thing signified. Every sign not only stands for what it stands for, but also stands for the absence of what it stands for."[18] Or even if the completely arepresentational Concrete poem is still a sign in communication, is it still a *rational* sign or is *that* precluded by the notion of the sign-as-absence? Recognized as an important aspect of signifying behavior (e.g., by Henri Meschonnic in *Le Signe et le poème* [Paris, 1975]), sign-as-absence

> has also been related to Freud's well-known analysis of the *fort-da* episode in child development, i.e., the stage where the child learns to reconcile itself with the *absence* of the mother. In certain kinds of schizophrenia there is an attempt to escape from the sign-as-absence, i.e., the patient reifies verbal signs to the extent that they no longer denote the *absence* of things signified, but the *presence* of themselves. They become "things" to be focused upon and played with in such schizophrenic activities as verbigeration and production of "word salad." Freud captures this pathological reification of verbal signs by saying that the patient hypercathects the *Wortvorstellung* at the expense of the *Dingvorstellung.* [Laferrière, p. 13]

Indeed, some Concrete poems—and those Computer poems

which aim to outdo Surrealist ones—are similar to schizo-phrenic writing (and may appear to be unintentionally imitat-ing it) when they contain many repetitions of few words or phrases and much asyntactic language. This similarity may sug-gest how arepresentational a poem can be before appearing to be an irrational sign in communication—or, put another way, how successful a poem *should* be in its "attempt to escape from the sign as an absence and to embrace the sign as an intensified presence of nothing but itself" (Laferrière, p. 13).

It is the Computer (rather than the Concrete) poem that is nothing but "an object in and by itself" even though the pro-grammer is trying to make the poem look not like such an object but like a traditional poem. And in Computer poetry, the collaboration between poet and reader becomes so fused that in the last step of the poetry-making process—selecting the best out of the computer's output—one cannot say whether the selector is functioning as the "poet" or as the "reader."

Poetry reading as play and supplying meaning can also be illustrated in a poem by Marc Adrian—a Concrete poem generated by a computer (see Fig. 3). Adrian does not admit that, here, the computer produces no semantic meaning for the spectator; instead, he comments that the "machine . . . allows the spectator to find his own meanings in the association of words more easily, since their choice, size, and disposition are determined at random." Program instructions for the poem were as follows:

1. Select combinations of words and syllables which make sense and which can be made from the following typographical ele-ments:
   ǀǀ oc (a vertical uninterrupted either above or below the line and a completed or an interrupted circle). . . Words could be in either German, English or French.
2. Select from storage twenty words at random.
3. Select at random a size for each of the words chosen—14, 36 or 84 point.[19]

Although this poem is both a Concrete and a Computer poem, it does not represent the evolution of the one into the other. Since it was composed six years after the poems of Auto-Beatnik, it represents the "doubling back," so to speak, of a Computer poem to simulate a Concrete poem, a creature of the *immediately preceding* species. This is in contrast to most Com-puter poetry, which actually attempts to "double back" to simu-

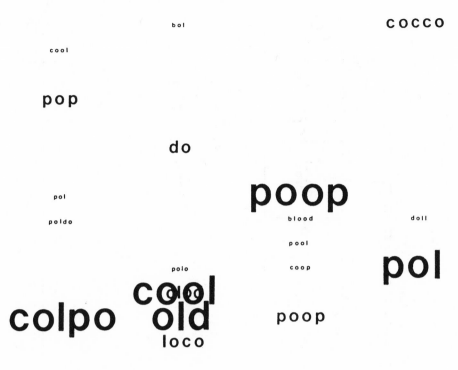

Fig. 3

Marc Adrian, *Computer Text.* Reprinted from *Cybernetic Serendipity: The Computer and the Arts,* ed. Jasia Reichardt (New York: Praeger, 1969). Copyright W. & J. Mackay & Co., Ltd., London, England, 1968.

late a *distant* predecessor, traditional poetry. (These species of poetry, as well as all those discussed above, are shown related in the "flow-chart" of Fig. 4.) Perhaps part of the difficulty that many readers experience in accepting Computer poetry as simulated traditional poetry is due to this property of "doubling back" too far, of trying to look like a species of poetry too remote in nature. A work that can be only an "object in and by itself" cannot succeed in appearing to be, as well, an "interpreter of exterior objects and . . . subjective feelings." On the other hand, I do not experience difficulty in accepting Adrian's

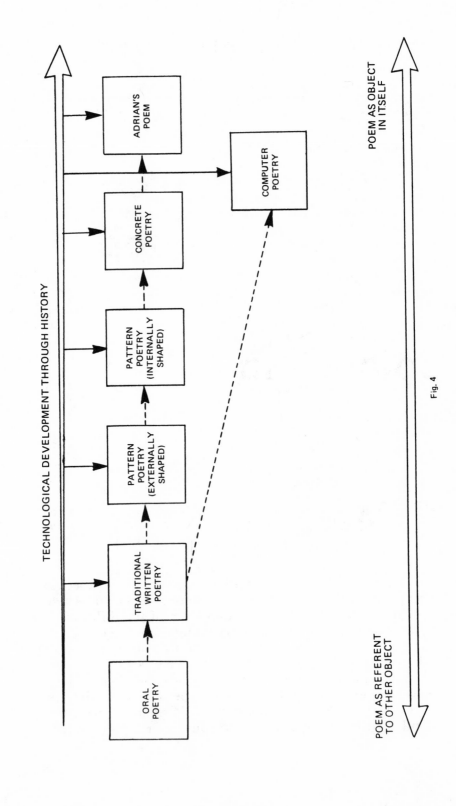

TECHNOLOGICAL DEVELOPMENT THROUGH HISTORY

ORAL POETRY

TRADITIONAL WRITTEN POETRY

PATTERN POETRY (EXTERNALLY SHAPED)

PATTERN POETRY (INTERNALLY SHAPED)

CONCRETE POETRY

ADRIAN'S POEM

COMPUTER POETRY

POEM AS REFERENT TO OTHER OBJECT

POEM AS OBJECT IN ITSELF

Fig. 4

poem—that is, in accepting Computer poetry as simulated Concrete poetry. Perhaps the reason is due to the property here of "doubling back" only to the nearest species, of a Computer poem trying to look like a species of poetry most similar to it in nature. A work that can be only an "object in and by itself" may succeed in being part of a work which is mostly an "object in and by itself."

For these reasons the most promising future for Computer poets may be not to continue refining the computer's ability to simulate traditional poetry but to develop the computer's use in helping to compose Concrete poetry—that is, to bring to Concrete poetry the computer's already advanced ability to produce graphic forms. Some of these forms—visual translations of complex mathematical formulas—have been acknowledged to possess "deep metaphysical beauty."[20] No one has ever said this about a Computer poem. Simpler but related graphic forms are already common in Concrete poetry, and so the genre might benefit greatly from the computer's integration of graphic forms with the words of the poet. The Concrete poet would create differently and perhaps better if he had a computer as his drawing instrument.

Perhaps, therefore, the line of poetic evolution that lies open for the computer is for its use in Concrete poetry to be developed into as richly graphic a use as has been developed for it in topology, design, engineering, and architecture. Then, instead of providing the poet with a storehouse of *words,* the computer could provide a storehouse of visual *forms* and—on the model of thesaurus, grammar book, and dictionary—could provide groupings of the visual forms into families, "syntaxes" of esthetic relationships among the forms, and semantic meanings associated with the forms in their use throughout history.[21] In this way, computer-assisted Concrete poems of the future might become such combinations of visual art and verbal meaning that they too would be said to possess "deep metaphysical beauty."

1. For the history of Pattern poetry, see Margaret Church, "The First English Pattern Poems," *PMLA* 61 (1946): 636–50; Charles Boultenhouse, "Poems in the Shapes of Things," *1959 Art News Annual 28,* Part 2 of *Art News* 57, no. 7 (November 1958): 65–83, 178; David W. Seaman, "The Development of Visual Poetry in France," *Visible Language* 6 (1972): 19–44; and my *Pattern Poetry: A Historical Critique from the Alexandrian Greeks to Dylan Thomas* (Boston: Marlborough House, 1976).

2. For the most comprehensive history of Concrete poetry, see the introduction to *Concrete Poetry: A World View*, ed. Mary Ellen Solt (Bloomington, Ind.: Indiana University Press, 1968).

3. See Howard Nemerov, "Speculative Equations: Poems, Poets, Computers," *American Scholar* 36 (1967): 394–414; Marie Borroff, "Creativity, Poetic Language, and the Computer," *Yale Review* 60 (1971): 481–513; Lesley Conger, "Off the Cuff: The Lesson of IBM 7094-7040 DCS," *The Writer* (October 1971), pp. 9–10; R. W. Bailey, "Computer-Assisted Poetry: The Writing Machine Is for Everybody," in *Computers in the Humanities*, ed. J. L. Mitchell (Minneapolis: University of Minnesota Press, 1974), pp. 283–95; and P. D. Juhl, "Do Computer Poems Show That an Author's Intention Is Irrelevant to the Meaning of a Literary Work?", *Critical Inquiry* 5 (1979): 481–87.

4. R. M. Worthy, "A New American Poet Speaks: The Works of A. B.," *Horizon* 4, no. 3 (1962): 96–99.

5. *The World of Abstract Art* (New York: George Wittenborn, n.d.), p. 37. Cited in Liselotte Gumpel, *Concrete Poetry from East and West Germany* (New Haven, Conn.: Yale University Press, 1976), p. 57. All concretist information is taken from Gumpel's book, cited hereafter in the text as Gumpel.

6. Francine Merritt, "Concrete Poetry—*Verbivocovisual*," *Speech Teacher* 18 (1969): 112.

7. The "Pilot Plan" is reprinted in *Concrete Poetry*, ed. Solt, pp. 71–72.

8. Edwin Morgan, "Note on Simulated Computer Poems," in *Cybernetic Serendipity: The Computer and the Arts*, ed. Jasia Reichardt (New York: Praeger, 1969), p. 57; copyright W. & J. Mackay & Co., Ltd., London, England, 1968; and Morgan's note to the poem in *An Anthology of Concrete Poetry*, ed. Emmett Williams (New York: Something Else Press, 1967).

9. Reprinted in *Concrete Poetry*, ed. Solt, pp. 78–80.

10. Here Gumpel is summarizing the procedure set forth in Max Bense, *Aesthetica: Einführung in die Aesthetik* (Baden-Baden: Agis-Verlag, 1965), pp. 208–25 and Max Bense, *Zeichen und Design: Semiotische Aesthetik* (Baden-Baden: Agis-Verlag, 1971), pp. 99–101, 106–7.

11. *Concrete Poetry*, ed. Solt, p. 15.

12. Ibid., pp. 58, 246, 309, and 310. See also Abbie W. Beiman, "Concrete Poetry: A Study in Metaphor," *Visible Language* 8 (1974): 217–18.

13. Eugen Gomringer, note to his poem "baum-kind-hund," in Williams, ed., *Anthology of Concrete Poetry*.

14. Gumpel is paraphrasing Helmut Heissenbüttel, *Über Literatur: Aufsätze und Frankfurter Vorlesungen* (Munich: Deutscher Taschenbuchverlag, 1970), pp. 221–24.

15. Eugen Gomringer, "From Line to Constellation," in *Concrete Poetry*, ed. Solt, p. 67. For Concrete poetry as play or game, see Gumpel, pp. 39–40, 141–43, and passim.

16. Augusto and Haroldo de Campos and Décio Pignatari, "Pilot Plan for Concrete Poetry," in *Concrete Poetry*, ed. Solt, p. 72.

17. Gumpel is paraphrasing Gomringer, *worte sind schatten: die konstellationen, 1951–1968*, ed. Helmut Heissenbüttel (Hamburg: Rowohlt, 1969), pp. 291–92.

18. Daniel Laferrière, *Sign and Subject: Semiotic and Psychoanalytic Investigations into Poetry* (Lisse: Peter de Ridder Press, 1978), p. 12, hereafter cited in the text as Laferrière.

19. In *Cybernetic Serendipity*, ed. Reichardt, p. 53.

20. Margaret Masterman and Robin McKinnon Wood, "The Poet and the Computer," *Times Literary Supplement*, 18 June 1970, p. 667.

21. The beginnings of such a storehouse are already available in book form. See, for instance, Peter S. Stevens, *Handbook of Regular Patterns: An Introduction to Symmetry in Two Dimensions* (Cambridge, Mass.: MIT Press, 1981), in which (according to the publisher's advertisement) "design patterns of many cultures and historical periods are categorized according to structure."